ANCIENT TRADITIONS— FUTURE POSSIBILITIES

Rhythmic Training Through the Traditions of Africa, Bali and India

by

Matthew Montfort

Panoramic Press
Mill Valley, California
1985

Address any correspondence to: Ancient Future Music,
POB 264, Kentfield CA 94914-0264

First edition, 1985.

Library of Congress Catalog Card Number: 86-60024

ISBN 0-937879-00-2

This publication is in partial fulfillment of the requirements for the masters degree in Arts and Media Technology, Mill Valley
Program, Antioch University West.

Degree and Review Committee Members:
    Matthew Montfort, B.A., Student
    Francis Coelho, Ph.D., A.U./W. Advisor
    Lynn Carpenter, M.A., Field Advisor
    David Schroeder, M.A., Field Advisor
    Lou Harrison, Composer/Musician/Teacher, Outside Expert

ACKNOWLEDGEMENTS

This work was completed after extensive research and study of the musical traditions of Africa, Bali and India. The author wishes to express thanks and gratitude to the following master musicians for their dedicated and caring instruction: I Madé Gerindem, Pak Sinti, Wayan Suweca, and I Komang Astita, all for instruction in Balinese gamelan; Ali Akbar Khan and Ram Narayan for instruction in North Indian music; and K.S. Subramanian and Guruvayoor Dorai for instruction in South Indian music. The author's studies in African music were guided by African and Latin percussionist Kim Atkinson. His help in locating all of the fine reference materials on African music was invaluable. The author wishes to thank all at the Ali Akbar College of Music and the Center for World Music. These two institutions are responsible for bringing a great many of the world's master musicians to the San Francisco Bay Area. Without the artistic climate created by this great influx of traditional musicians, this work would not have come about. The author wishes to thank the masters of North Indian rhythm, Alla Rakha and Zakir Hussain, for inspiring this work.

The following people are cited for contributions beyond the call of duty: Francis Coelho, for his consultations and guidance through every step of the process of creating this work from the original idea to publication; Benjy Wertheimer, for his help in proofreading, editing and compiling information for the section on North Indian rhythm; Marco Zonka, for his help in compiling information for the section on North Indian rhythm; Doug Vurek, for consultations on South Indian rhythm; George Ruckert, for his help in the author's North Indian music education and for his class in North Indian rhythm at the Ali Akbar College of Music; Mindy Klein, for her participation in the author's study trip to Bali; Rick Henderson, for proofreading and criticism; Ernie Mansfield, for music typesetting; Musica Engraving, for music typesetting; Paul Coelho, for text typesetting; Adriana Delma, for editing and proofreading; Michael Reibin, for camera and press work; Charles Montfort, for his support; and Connie Montfort, for her support.

TABLE OF CONTENTS

INTRODUCTION

This book is designed to fill a need for basic rhythmic training through the study of the rhythmic traditions of Africa, Bali and India. While European classical music emphasized the development of harmony, musicians in cultures such as those of Africa, Bali and India developed rhythm to a very advanced degree. Today, there is an increasing interest among contemporary Western musicians in expanding their awareness of these great oral traditions. Jazz, jazz-rock and contemporary classical music have been absorbing many ethnic musical influences through the work of such artists as Don Cherry, John McLaughlin, Oregon, Paul Winter Consort, Do'a, Terry Riley, Steve Reich, and the author's own ensemble, Ancient Future. Contemporary musicians have a unique opportunity to broaden their knowledge and skills through studying the music of cultures foreign to their upbringing.

For the professional musician, ability with rhythm is essential. Yet, it is often the last thing one thinks of studying. Many people think of rhythm as a natural ability as opposed to something that can be developed. The notion that one either "has it" or doesn't is a common misconception about rhythm, and is often used as an excuse not to try to improve. It is simply a matter of refining one's rhythmic sense through practice.

By concentrating on the unique aspects of the traditions of Africa, Bali and India, this work strives to form a matrix of rhythmic knowledge that will be of use to the contemporary performer and composer. The purpose is not to aid the student in mastering any one tradition, but rather to give the student a broad base of rhythmic knowledge and skill from which to draw upon. From this base, the rhythmic knowledge of any tradition will be more immediately accessible.

Through these ancient traditions, this work also seeks to point a way towards new musical directions and innovations. We have come to a turning point in the evolution of music. The technology of communications has had the effect of making the music of the whole earth readily available. One needs to go no further than the local record store to find music from Africa, Asia, Europe, Indonesia, the Middle East and South America. At the same time, modern rock music has become very popular in third world countries. However, as industrialization takes its toll on traditional ways of life, the social structures for traditional music are changing, causing some forms of music to become endangered species. Efforts to preserve music in its traditional state can cause performances to take on a "museum-like" character, rewarding the status quo instead of innovation. While the preservation of our heritages is very important, traditions that are afraid to change have a tendency to become stagnant, and this can kill their vitality just as surely as neglect. The world needs both the enriching effect of the preservation of its musical heritages and the stimulating effect of new innovations.

There is an abundance of musical knowledge available to the musician with a global perspective. European classical music has developed harmony, polyphony and orchestration to an advanced state. Indian music has developed melody and rhythm to a high degree of refinement. African music has developed multiple layers of rhythm into an advanced form. Balinese music has developed a refined form of orchestral percussion with interlocking rhythmic phrases. This ancient musical knowledge can continue as a vital part of contemporary and future music through the development of *world fusion music*, music that combines ideas from many of the earth's traditions. Imagine the artistic possibilities for new music that draws upon such a rich and varied palette for its inspiration!

The groundwork has already been laid for the development of world fusion music. As early as 1964, the recording *Music for Zen Meditation* was released, on which jazz clarinetist Tony Scott played with Japanese classical musicians, who accompanied him on shakuhachi and koto. Ravi Shankar, the North Indian sitar master, has recorded with such varied musical personalities as classical violinist Yehudi Menuhin and former Beatle George Harrison. Such experimental collaborations show us a good deal about the process of cultural exchange. "In order to be able to play a 'music between the worlds' capable of linking up these worlds into a single, integral entity," writes German composer Peter Michael Hamel in his book *Through Music to the Self*, "completely new modes of music making need to be developed alongside the ancient methods still in the process of rediscovery. In order to permit a jazz musician, for example, to fit in with an Asian improviser, both need

1

to familiarize themselves with the typical playing techniques and idiosyncrasies of the other. Through confronting the strange and unknown—often, indeed, initially a subject for mirth— the individual learns to recognize that his own method, hitherto imagined to be the obvious, or even the 'only' method, is in fact only one method *among many*, one possibility *among many*."[1] Indeed, groups such as Shakti, featuring virtuoso guitarist John McLaughlin, South Indian violin master L. Shankar, South Indian master percussionist T.H. Vinayakram and North Indian tabla master Zakir Hussain, have come a long way towards presenting a format in which each musician understands the other's tradition and each can offer his own unique contribution to the musical whole. McLaughlin, long intrigued by Indian music, took time out of his busy schedule over a period of years to study Indian music intensively. In the process of forming Shakti, Shankar learned harmonic theory from McLaughlin while Shankar further schooled McLaughlin in South Indian music. Zakir Hussain and T.H. Vinayakram each had to stretch to learn the drumming styles of the other, for North Indian and South Indian music are different traditions. The resulting music combined the highest expression of each performer in a ground-breaking synthesis of East and West.

The matrix of rhythmic knowledge formed by this work offers the composer and improvising musician a wealth of material from which to draw upon for inspiration. Learn the material presented in this work, and once it is mastered, it may become a part of one's musical expression. Additional rhythms may be created by combining the traditional rhythms of Africa, Bali and India. Examples of a few of the possible combinations are given in the final chapter of this work. These hybrid rhythm exercises and the traditional rhythms are valuable learning aids and may provide the inspiration for compositions and improvisations of world fusion music.

[1]Peter Michael Hamel, *Through Music to the Self*, (London: Compton Press, 1978), 136.

HOW TO USE THIS BOOK

This book is organized in two sections. Section I, entitled *Ancient Traditions*, is divided into three chapters. Chapter 1 is devoted to the rhythms of West Africa, Chapter 2 is devoted to the rhythms of Bali, and Chapter 3 to the rhythms of India. Great care was taken to present this material as accurately as possible.[1] Aspects of the cultures from which the musical traditions were born are also discussed as much as space permits. Section II, entitled *Future Possibilities*, is a brief introduction to some of the new directions and innovations made possible by cross-cultural exchange.

The exercises in each chapter are divided into groups. Each exercise group develops a specific rhythmic aspect or skill. The exercises are further divided between those that develop individual skills and those that develop skills in ensemble playing. The ensemble exercises require additional players and are ideal for classroom and workshop situations. A personal multi-track tape recorder would allow one to practice the exercises without other players, but is no substitute for ensemble experience. Form a study group with friends, or if there is a lack of suitable partners, put up ads and notices about town.

An attempt has been made to present the material in its order of difficulty within each chapter. However, for the sake of continuity it was necessary to present some difficult material early in each chapter. Some of the material is extremely advanced and may take repeated practice over a long period of time to master. Unless otherwise indicated, the student may read ahead past a difficult exercise, reviewing it often while simultaneously working on new exercises.

An attempt should be made to approach these exercises with an open mind. One should not make assumptions about the traditions being studied based on previous experience with other forms of music. The basic rhythmic concepts of African music, for instance, are quite different from those of European music.

The exercises in this book can be performed with a minimum of materials. There is no need to learn new instrumental techniques, for most of the exercises can be performed with only the hands, vocal chords and body. The use of instruments is optional. It is recommended that the student purchase a good metronome. Start each exercise at a comfortable and slow tempo, and then gradually bring the pace up to the tempo indicated. If there is no metronome speed indicated, perform the exercise at a tempo that seems appropriate.

The exercises are written in Western music notation and concentrate on the rhythmic aspects of the traditions covered. While melody is generally not the concern of this particular work, in some cases, such as in Balinese music, it is inseparable from the rhythmic material being presented and is thus included.

Before proceeding to the main body of this work, a definition of the terms that will be used throughout the work is in order. There are basic aspects of rhythm which are common to all of the traditions presented in this book. Generally speaking within the field of music, *rhythm* can be defined as everything pertaining to the timing and duration of musical sounds. Three of the most basic aspects of rhythm are time, movement in time, and the presence or lack of a strict regularity of movement in time. Music with strict regularity of movement in time is said to have *pulse*, and music without pulse is said to be in *free rhythm*. This work concentrates exclusively on music which has pulse. For the purposes of this work, a *beat* is defined as the basic unit used to measure musical time. A beat ranges from short to long in duration,[2] but within any section of music the duration

---

[1]Accuracy is not an easy task, for in a land with such geographical and cultural differences as India, for instance, there are many schools of thought, each with its own peculiarities. In the field of ethnomusicology, one must learn to take absolute statements cautiously, for a living musical tradition can produce almost as many exceptions as rules.

[2]The human ear can start to distinguish separate distinct pulses at an upper limit of about twenty pulses per second. The lower limit varies with training. Some musicians are able to execute regular periods of a minute or more with precision.

of the beat is constant unless there is a change of tempo. *Tempo* may be defined as the speed of the beats within a section of music. The metronome tempo markings indicate the number of beats per minute. A beat may be subdivided into a number of counts or smaller beats. For the purposes of this work, a *count* is defined as unit of musical time, usually used to count the number of divisions per beat. A *measure* is a section of music between two bar lines. The term *meter* refers to the basic grouping of beats and accents within a measure. *Offbeat* refers to a point between beats. *Down beat* refers to the first beat of the measure. A glossary appears at the end of each chapter, covering any new terms introduced.

Terms from the musical cultures presented in this work are italicized in the text. To simplify the task of the reader, the plural forms of these italicized terms are created by adding an ''s'' at the end of the word as if they were words in the English language. Terms utilized in Western music which may be new to the reader are italicized where they are first defined, and thereafter are set in normal text.

Enjoy the material presented in this book and review it often. It is hoped that this work will inspire musicians to find out more about the traditional music of the world and to further their own musical identities in the process.

SECTION I

ANCIENT TRADITIONS

CHAPTER 1
WEST AFRICA

Multiple Layers of Rhythm

In West Africa, tribal societies such as the *Yoruba*, the *Eve*, the *Akan* and the *Ibo* possess a music rich in rhythmic vitality. It is a music of multiple layers of rhythms. While European classical music has developed complex harmonies of tones, African music has developed a complex interweaving of contrasting rhythmic patterns. The African strives for the occurrence of at least two different rhythms at once, and it is precisely this juxtaposition of opposing rhythms that creates the vital spark of African music.

In many West African societies, music and dance have developed as a part of community life. They are performed for recreational activities, ceremonies, rites or collective activities such as building bridges, clearing paths or putting out fires. This is not to imply that music is performed for every occasion. For instance, some societies prefer to celebrate weddings with an abundance of music, while others do not include music in the ceremony.[1] The musicians, dancers and spectators all work together to make the occasion a success. The musicians time their rhythmic variations to inspire the dancers before they show obvious signs of waning vigor. Dancers also have a responsibility to the musicians. For example, if the music is not being played well, the dancers may simplify their steps in order to emphasize a more basic rhythm. Africans expect the music to be responsive to the development of the social setting. To quote African music scholar John Miller Chernoff, "When you ask an African how he enjoyed certain music, he may very well respond by saying, 'It was a beautiful scene.' He understands that the music is important only in respect to the overall success of a social occasion, and he does not focus on the music but rather on the way the situation is picked up by the music."[2]

The concept of time in African music has a different emphasis than that of the West. The rhythmic framework of European classical music can be generally thought of as a succession of notes and harmonies moving through time at a unified pace towards a predetermined end, whereas the African approach to rhythm does not limit itself to one meter at a time. Different rhythmic patterns move on seemingly different tracks to be part of the kaleidoscope of sound that is African rhythm. The music starts, sets up layers of interconnecting rhythms, the parts repeat or shift to new patterns creating new peaks, until at some point the music comes to a stop.

In listening to African music for the first time, it is often hard for Westerners to "find the beat" in the maze of sound. Perhaps this is due to the fact that the unifying principle of African music is not a basic pulse that permeates everything, but rather a larger *time span*[3]. This fixed time span is delineated by a repeating pattern that is usually played on a metal bell. The time span may be divided into equal pulses (accordingly this principle is known as *divisive* rhythm). If the time span is divided into groups of two, four, eight, or sixteen pulses, the passage is in *duple* meter, and if the time span is divided into groups of three, six, twelve, or twenty-four pulses, the passage is in *triple* meter.

[1]J.H. Kwabena Nketia, *The Music of Africa*, (New York: W.W. Norton and Company, 1974), 21-34.

[2]John Miller Chernoff, *African Rhythm and African Sensibility*, (Chicago: University of Chicago Press, 1979), 67.

[3]J.H. Kwabena Nketia, *The Music of Africa*, (New York: W.W. Norton and Company, 1974), 126.

TIME SPAN

[--]

DUPLE METER

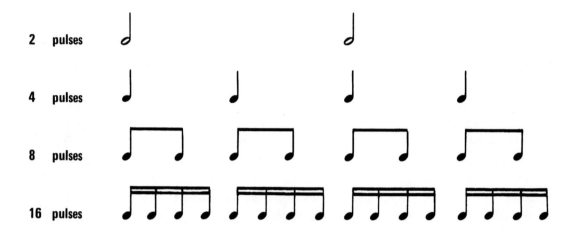

2 pulses

4 pulses

8 pulses

16 pulses

TRIPLE METER

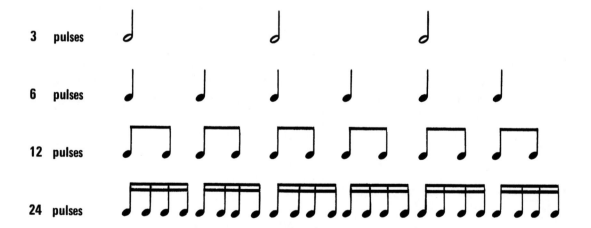

3 pulses

6 pulses

12 pulses

24 pulses

Alternating sections of duple and triple time are also common in African music. This phenomenon is known as *hemiola*. In notation of African rhythms, duple meter is often written utilizing dotted quarter notes in 6/8 or 12/8 time instead of quarter notes in 2/4 or 4/4 time to show the time relationship of the duple meter sections to the triple meter sections.

HEMIOLA

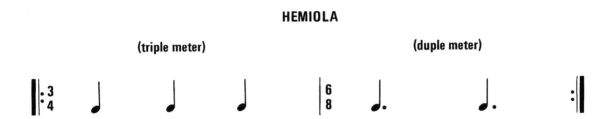

Unequal groupings of pulses can be phrased together to add up to the time span. Such groupings are known as *additive* rhythms. For example, the groupings of $3 + 3 + 2$ adding up to eight pulses and $2 + 3 + 2 + 2 + 3$ adding up to 12 pulses are both common in African music.

ADDITIVE RHYTHMS

3 + 3 + 2

2 + 3 + 2 + 2 + 3

| 1 2 3 | 1 2 3 | 1 2 | | 1 2 | 1 2 3 | 1 2 | 1 2 | 1 2 3 |

Certain players in the ensemble may divide the time span into duple meter while at the same time others divide it into triple meter, creating *multiple meter*. Each player unifies his part with the bell pattern, which is one cycle of the time span in length. Often, the bell pattern is an additive rhythm, a very common form being $2 + 2 + 1 + 2 + 2 + 2 + 1$ in 12/8.

BELL PATTERN

1 2 1 2 1 1 2 1 2 1 2 1

A basic pulse of six quarter notes or four dotted quarters will fit equally well with such a bell pattern, allowing each player to unify his part with the same pattern and yet maintain his own meter.

MULTIPLE METER

The juxtaposition of additive and divisive rhythms (such as the bell pattern and four equal pulses) creates complex *cross rhythms*, as does the juxtaposition of duple and triple meter. Contrasts in the tones of the interlocking rhythms form a pattern heard as a *resultant*. The African musician may keep the resultant pattern in mind to help him maintain the cross-rhythmic relationship with the other part.

RESULTANT RHYTHM

The effect of all this is music of great polyrhythmic interplay. It's no wonder that some Westerners have trouble "finding the beat", as there are typically two or more meters present! A.M. Jones, one of the foremost African music scholars, put it very well when he wrote, "We have to grasp the fact that that if from childhood you are brought up to regard beating three against two as being just as normal as beating in synchrony, then you develop a two-dimensional attitude to rhythm which we in the West do not share."[4]

The Westerner studying African rhythm must learn to listen to at least two rhythms at once, for only through the combined rhythms does the music emerge. Many musicians would greatly benefit from developing this two-dimensional approach to rhythm as a part of their basic skills. It is toward the realization of this goal that the exercises in this chapter were created. Western musicians may find it helpful to think about African rhythms in terms that are familiar to them, and for this reason the exercises were written in Western notation. It is important, however, to take into consideration that Africans have an oral traditon, learning these rhythms by ear and through exposure to them throughout childhood. One should not jump to conclusions about African music based on one's own different concepts of rhythm. For instance, the issue of what is "on the beat" or "off the beat" may become cloudy in music of multiple meters. Within this work, the relationship between each part and the bell pattern is shown by notating everything in measures equal to one cycle of the bell pattern. Since each player may be keeping his own subjective beat in relationship to the bell pattern, a part may be on the offbeat in relationship to the time signature written while being precisely on the beat that the player is keeping in relationship to the bell pattern. If one counts two against three in 3/4 time, each beat of the three falls on the beat, yet the second beat of the two falls on the offbeat.

TWO AGAINST THREE

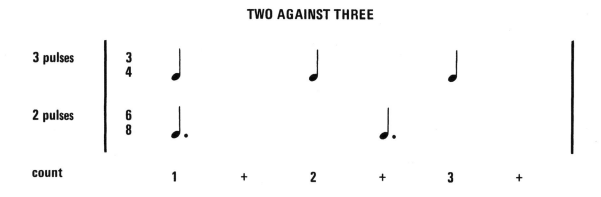

Considering all of this, it is better to think of an additive rhythm as a set of groupings of two's and three's than as a syncopated passage, with accents "on" and "off" the beat.

NOTATION COMPARISON

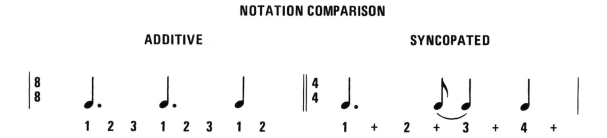

[4]A.M. Jones, *Studies in African Music*, (London: Oxford University Press, 1957), I, 102.

To gain better insight into the African concept of rhythm, it is important to look at how the African is trained as a musician. "A crying African child," writes John Miller Chernoff, "is attracted and soothed by lullabies with rhythms that cut across the rhythm of the arms which rock and comfort him."[5] The African mother sings to her child in syllables imitative of drum rhythms. When he is of sufficient age, he learns to imitate these rhythms by rote. Children are given toy drums upon which to tap out rhythms, often as soon as they can control their arms.[6] In African languages, proper rhythmic phrasing and accentuation are essential to meaning, and children's songs and games display an advanced rhythmic character. A young boy may sit beside his father at a musical event, tapping out rhythms on the side of a drum as his father plays on the drum head.[7] Adolescents play minor roles in adult ensembles, and as they become more proficient their roles may expand. The organization of music within the society encourages musicians to acquire musical knowledge in slow stages through participation in social and musical activities.[8]

Social cooperation has made its impact on the African concept of time. As John Miller Chernoff maintains, "Rhythms are built into the way people relate to each other. When women pound cooked yams, the woman who turns the yams while her friends are rhythmically smashing them with heavy wooden poles converses most amiably, as if the safety of her fingers were of no concern. Obviously she does not have to try very hard to maintain a simple rhythm, and she counts on her friends to be just as steady."[9] Musicians depend just as heavily on the rhythmic ability of the other players. Often an African musician will have difficulty playing his variations without the presence of a counter-rhythm. The very thing that would tend to throw Western musicians off of the beat is regarded by the African as being the only thing that keeps him in time, for in African music, one rhythm defines another. When someone is just learning African music, he may be told to concentrate only on his part, lest he be thrown off by the other rhythms. This may be a valuable stage for the student to go through, but it is just that—a stage. Once one has reached the level of musicianship required to be able to play in an ensemble situation, it becomes easier to hear one's part when the whole ensemble is playing.

This interdependence between players in the ensemble requires an advanced set of rhythmic skills. With the growing use of polyrhythms in modern music, ensemble skills are of paramount importance to today's musician. Through studying African rhythm, contemporary musicians may acquire the ensemble-oriented rhythmic ability that generations of West African musicians have developed.

[5]John Miller Chernoff, *African Rhythm and African Sensibility*, (Chicago: University of Chicago Press, 1979), 94.

[6]J.H Kwabena Nketia, *The Music of Africa*, (New York: W.W. Norton and Company, 1974), 60.

[7]John Miller Chernoff, *African Rhythm and African Sensibility*, (Chicago: University of Chicago Press, 1979), 94.

[8]J.H Kwabena Nketia, *The Music of Africa*, (New York: W.W. Norton and Company, 1974), 63.

[9]John Miller Chernoff, *African Rhythm and African Sensibility*, (Chicago: University of Chicago Press, 1979), 94.

AFRICAN RHYTHM EXERCISES

The exercises in this chapter fall into two categories: those that require two or more partners, and those that can be practiced alone. Because this music is based on multiple layers of rhythm, the two-part exercises designed for individual practice are of extra benefit when divided between two partners. Conversely, all parts of multiple-partner exercises should be thoroughly explored by each musician before a run-through is attempted. Practice each exercise slowly at first and gradually work up to a faster pace.

There is much controversy among scholars about the written notation of African music; some utilize Western notation while others claim that African music cannot be adequately represented without the development of an entirely new notation system. Because the purpose of this book is to make some of this knowledge more accessible to Western musicians, the rhythms have been written in Western notation. One should be careful not to jump to conclusions about traditional African music based on the conventions of the Western music notation system. For instance, in European classical music, the implied accents (unless otherwise stated) in a four-beat meter are on the first and third beat. It would be erroneous to assume that the same were true in African music, for the African tends to accent the second and fourth beat in such a configuration.

To adapt the Western notation system to African rhythms, a number of different devices have been employed. All of the parts are barred according to the time span of the bell pattern in order to show a unifying principle. Phrasing marks are used to show groupings that cross bar lines. Because of the predominance of additive rhythms, the use of ties has been avoided (except across bar lines) through the use of dotted notes.

Language plays a very important role in African music, and has been utilized in the exercises presented in this chapter. Onomatopeia, the development of syllables to imitate sounds, is quite prevalent in African music. These syllables are used extensively in learning drum music. In talking drum music, drums imitate actual words so faithfully that communication using only drums is possible. The African normally learns the drum syllables simultaneously with the music. In the interest of presenting this rhythmic knowledge to Western musicians, recitation is first introduced with familiar Western numerals and then with traditional African syllables.

The following exercises are structured in a series of steps that lead up to mastery of each rhythm. The African musician does not learn the rhythms in the manner presented here; he learns through a process of assimilating the cultural and musical knowledge present in his environment. Western musicians learn these African rhythms from a different vantage point, and tend to need to break the rhythms down into their component parts in order to thoroughly understand them. This step is natural and often necessary, but once a rhythm is mastered there is great benefit to be gained by concentrating upon the feel of the rhythm rather than its component parts.

The exercises presented here can be used as an introduction to African rhythmic concepts. Mastery of them should be helpful to one's musicianship, whatever one's musical goals may be.

EXERCISE I

Hemiola

The alternation of duple and triple meters, or hemiola, is a common feature of African rhythm.

A. Practice alternating between triple and duple meter by using a common pulse of six eighth notes as a guide. Start by reciting the count alone, then add the top rhythm by tapping it out on the thighs or a table.

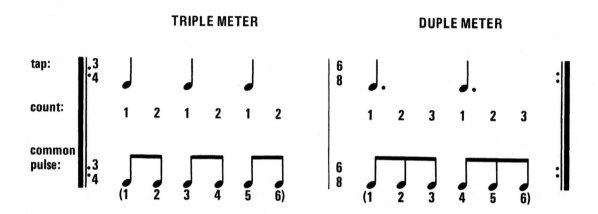

B. Alter the recitation of the count by reciting one number per quarter note in the 3/4 section and then doubling the count in the 6/8 section to one number per eighth note as follows:

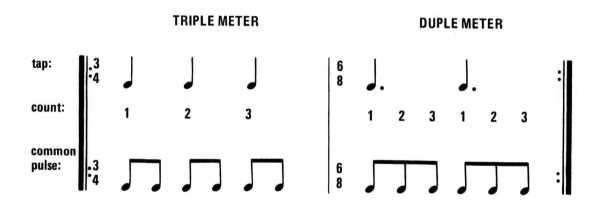

C. Finally, recite one number per eighth note in the 3/4 section and one number per dotted eighth in the 6/8 section to experience the "feel" of alternating duple and triple meter. Start with a slow tempo and gradually increase the speed.

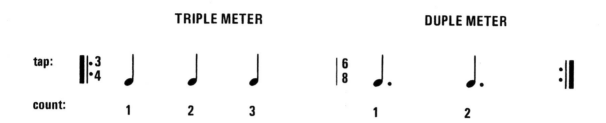

D. Then switch the order, playing duple meter followed by triple meter. Alternate between duple and triple meter in various combinations until it is possible to switch between them at will.

EXERCISE II

Additive Rhythms

Additive rhythms, asymmetrical combinations of groups of two and three pulses, are a characteristic element of African music. A thorough grasp of additive rhythms is essential to the student of African rhythm.

A. The following rhythm is a standard pattern that occurs in much African and Afro-American music. Become familiar with the basic pattern by tapping it out while counting the pulse divisions out loud. Practice alternating between the variations after learning each one individually.

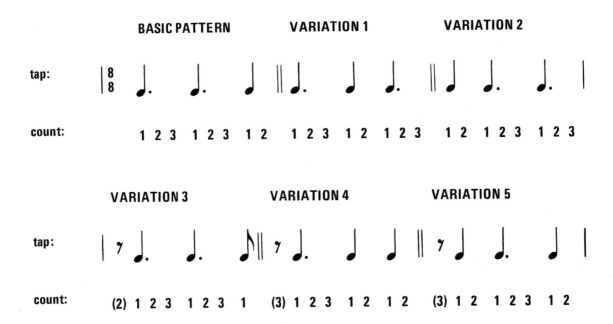

Many different additive rhythms can be formed by combining groups of two's and three's over several time spans. The following rhythm is common, not only in African music, but in Latin American and Indian music as well. It can be formed by combining Variation 4 with the basic pattern. Experiment with different combinations of the above variations.

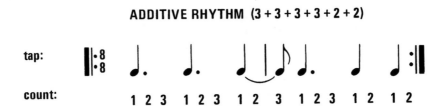

B. The following rhythm is a standard bell pattern that is prevalent in African music.

16

The bell pattern is a cyclic form, and may begin anywhere in its cycle. There are therefore four main variations, each beginning on one of the notes of the original pattern.

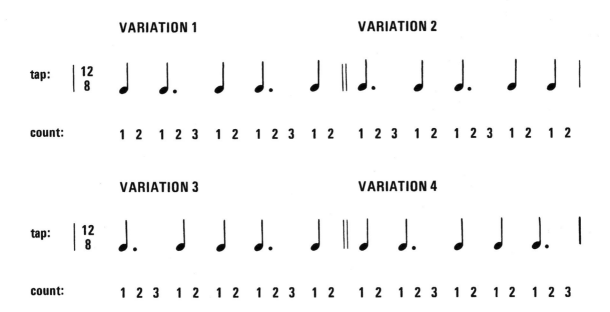

VARIATION 1   VARIATION 2

tap: 12/8

count: 1 2 1 2 3 1 2 1 2 3 1 2   1 2 3 1 2 1 2 3 1 2 1 2

VARIATION 3   VARIATION 4

tap: 12/8

count: 1 2 3 1 2 1 2 1 2 3 1 2   1 2 1 2 3 1 2 1 2 1 2 3

By substituting a quarter note and an eighth note for each dotted quarter note, many additional variations of the standard bell pattern are possible. The following two patterns are common variations. Experiment with creating other variations.

PATTERN 1   PATTERN 2

tap: 12/8

count: 1 2 1 2 1 1 2 1 2 1 2 1   1 2 1 2 1 2 1 1 2 1 2 1

EXERCISE III

Bi-Rhythms

A. The rhythmic feeling of two against three is very prominent in African music. The following is a step-by-step method to gain mastery of this bi-rhythm. The steps may be repeated as necessary or spread over several days.

1. Count the numbers in the middle column out loud, tapping with the left hand on one, and with the right hand on one, three and five.

LEFT HAND	COUNT	RIGHT HAND
1	1	1
	2	
	3	3
	4	
	5	5
	6	

2. Then tap on one and four with the left hand while tapping on one with the right hand.

LEFT HAND	COUNT	RIGHT HAND
1	1	1
	2	
	3	
4	4	
	5	
	6	

3. Combine steps 1 and 2.

LEFT HAND	COUNT	RIGHT HAND
1	1	1
	2	
	3	3
4	4	
	5	5
	6	

4. The next step is to transfer one's awareness from a feeling of six pulses to one of two pulses with the left hand against three pulses with the right. Tap out the same pulses as in step 3, but this time count out loud only the pulses of the right hand.

LEFT HAND	COUNT	RIGHT HAND
1	1	1
.	.	.
.	2	2
2	.	.
.	3	3
.	.	.

5. Then count out the pulses of the left hand while tapping three pulses with the right hand and two pulses with the left hand, as follows:

LEFT HAND	COUNT	RIGHT HAND
1	1	1
.	.	.
.	.	2
2	2	.
.	.	3
.	.	.

6. Keeping a slow tempo, alternate between step 4 and step 5 until it is possible to switch between them at will. This is similar to switching between the two perspectives of an Escher print.

B. Use the same techniques presented for mastering two against three to master three against four. Abbreviate the pronunciation of two-syllable numbers to avoid counting them as two pulses.

LEFT HAND	COUNT	RIGHT HAND
1	1	1
	2	
	3	
	4	4
5	5	
	6	
	7 (sev')	7
	8	
9	9	
	10	10
	11 ('lev')	
	12	

UNIVERSAL BI-RHYTHM RULE

These same techniques can be used to master any bi-rhythm. To figure out the number of pulses to be counted out loud, multiply the number of pulses to be tapped by the left hand, which will be designated x, times the number of pulses to be tapped by the right hand, which will be designated y. Starting on the first pulse of the total number of pulses to be counted out loud (x X y), the left hand will tap every y number of pulses and the right hand will tap every x number of pulses.

The following bi-rhythms are given as examples of the Universal Bi-Rhythm Rule.

1.   THREE AGAINST FIVE

LEFT HAND	COUNT	RIGHT HAND
1	1	1
	2	
	3	
	4	4
	5	
6	6	
	7	7
	8	
	9	
	10	1 0
11	11	
	12	
	13	1 3
	14	
	15	

2.   THREE AGAINST SEVEN

LEFT HAND	COUNT	RIGHT HAND
1	1	1
	2	
	3	
	4	4
	5	
	6	
	7	7
8	8	
	9	
	10	10
	11	
	12	
	13	13
	14	
15	15	
	16	16
	17	
	18	
	19	19
	20	
	21	

3. FOUR AGAINST FIVE

LEFT HAND	COUNT	RIGHT HAND
1	1	1
	2	
	3	
	4	
	5	5
6	6	
	7	
	8	
	9	9
	10	
11	11	
	12	
	13	1 3
	14	
	15	
16	16	
	17	1 7
	18	
	19	
	20	

4.   FOUR AGAINST SEVEN

LEFT HAND	COUNT	RIGHT HAND
1	1	1
	2	
	3	
	4	
	5	5
	6	
	7	
8	8	
	9	9
	10	
	11	
	12	
	13	1 3
	14	
15	15	
	16	
	17	1 7
	18	
	19	
	20	
	21	2 1
22	22	
	23	
	24	
	25	2 5
	26	
	27	
	28	

EXERCISE IV

Additive and divisive rhythms often occur simultaneously in African music. This exercise deals with learning to keep a steady pulse against the additive rhythms covered in Exercise II by tapping out a divisive rhythm with one hand and an additive rhythm with the other. Count the rhythms out loud, alternating between the divisive rhythm and the pulse divisions of the additive rhythm. Each part of this exercise is written both in standard notation and in chart form to aid in visualizing the rhythm. In the charts, taps are indicated by an "X", pauses by a "–".

A.   **8/8 METER**

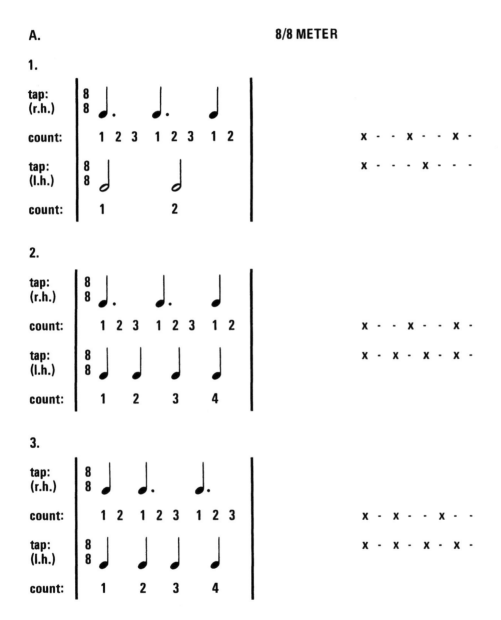

4.

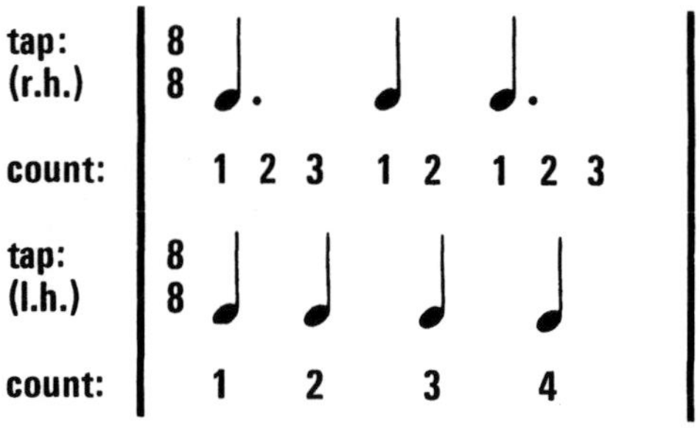

tap: (r.h.) 8/8 ♩.   ♩   ♩.

count: 1 2 3 1 2 1 2 3

x - - x - x - -

tap: (l.h.) 8/8 ♩   ♩   ♩   ♩

x - x - x - x -

count: 1   2   3   4

5.

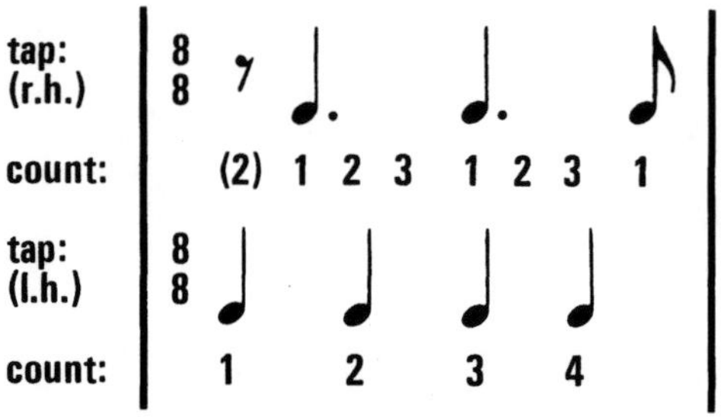

tap: (r.h.) 8/8 𝄾 ♩.   ♩.   ♪

count: (2) 1 2 3 1 2 3 1

- x - - x - - x

tap: (l.h.) 8/8 ♩   ♩   ♩   ♩

x - x - x - x -

count: 1   2   3   4

6.

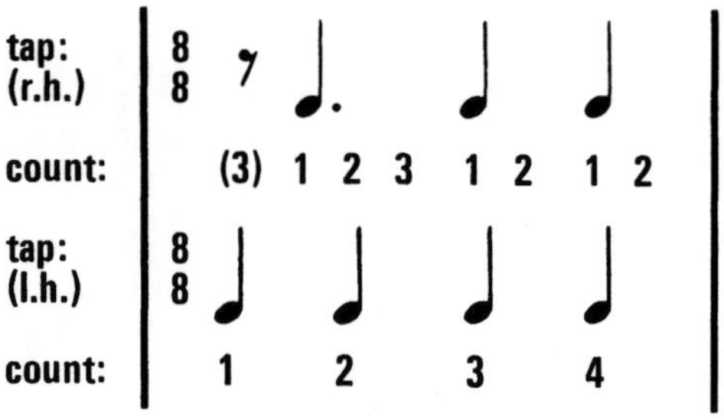

tap: (r.h.) 8/8 𝄾 ♩.   ♩   ♩

count: (3) 1 2 3 1 2 1 2

- x - - x - x -

tap: (l.h.) 8/8 ♩   ♩   ♩   ♩

x - x - x - x -

count: 1   2   3   4

7.

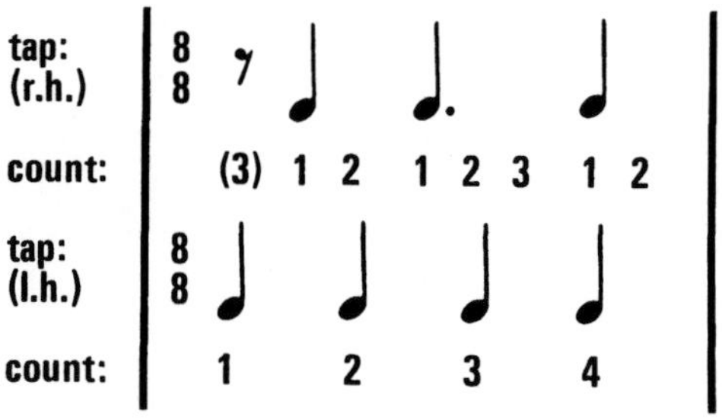

tap: (r.h.) 8/8 𝄾 ♩   ♩.   ♩

count: (3) 1 2 1 2 3 1 2

- x - x - - x -

tap: (l.h.) 8/8 ♩   ♩   ♩   ♩

x - x - x - x -

count: 1   2   3   4

8.

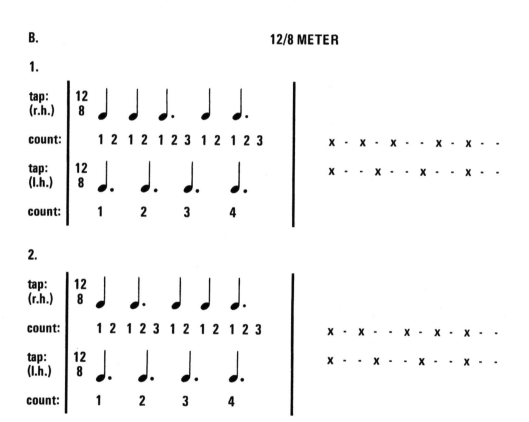

X – – X – – X – – X – – X – X –

X – X – X – X – X – X – X – X –

B.   **12/8 METER**

1.

x - x - x - - x - x - -

x - - x - - x - - x - -

2.

x - x - - x - x - x - -

x - - x - - x - - x - -

27

3.

tap: (r.h.)	$\frac{12}{8}$ ♩ ♩ ♪♩ ♩ ♩ ♪	x - x - x x - x - x - x
count:	1 2 1 2 1 1 2 1 2 1 2 1	
tap: (l.h.)	$\frac{12}{8}$ ♩. ♩. ♩. ♩.	x - - x - - x - - x - -
count:	1 2 3 4	

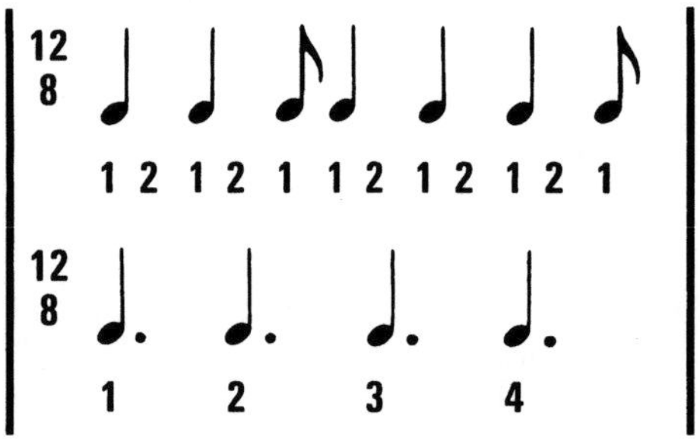

4.

tap: (r.h.)	$\frac{12}{8}$ ♩ ♩ ♪♩ ♩ ♩ ♪	x - x - x x - x - x - x
count:	1 2 1 2 1 1 2 1 2 1 2 1	
tap: (l.h.)	$\frac{12}{8}$ ♩ ♩ ♩ ♩ ♩ ♩	x - x - x - x - x - x -
count:	1 2 3 4 5 6	

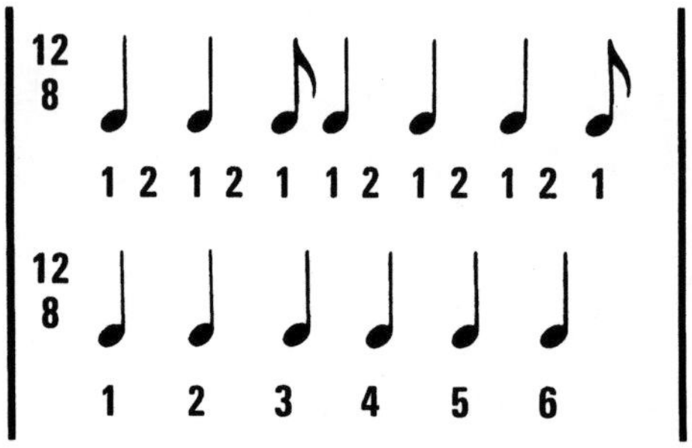

EXERCISE V

Resultants

    While the African musician plays a bi-rhythm, he keeps in mind the resultant rhythm produced by the two parts when played together. Learn each of the following bi-rhythms and then play the two parts simultaneously to produce the resultant rhythm. While keeping both parts going, alternate between counting out the first part, the second part and the resultant rhythm.

A.   8/8 METER

1. Following the above directions will help the reader to understand the African concept of offset spacing of the same rhythm which differs from the Western concept of beats and offbeats.

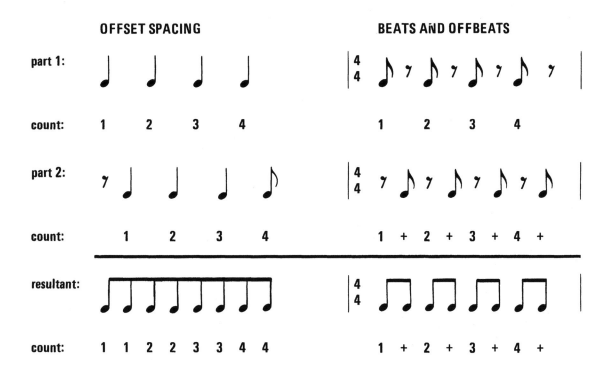

COUNT ALTERNATION

2. This rhythm is a combination of two against three in the first half of the measure, and straight four in the second half. It is an excellent exercise in switching feels from triple to duple. The top line is an interesting bell pattern, while the second line claps an even four.

BELL PATTERN

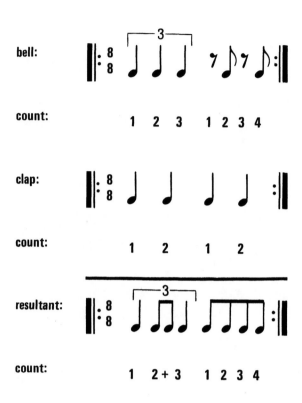

3. This exercise combines two against three in the first half of the measure with the additive pattern 3 + 3 + 2 in the second half. It is very useful for developing a sense of the difference between a triplet and the 3 + 3 + 2 pattern.

TRIPLET AND ADDITIVE PATTERN COMPARED

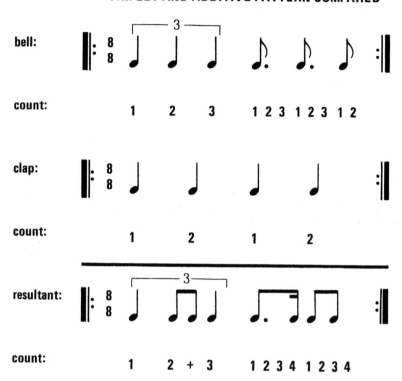

B.   **12/8 METER**

1. This rhythm is from the music of the *Ibo* people[10] and is performed by one person on a pair of shakers. Each shaker plays a variation of the standard bell pattern rhythm, and the resultant is also a variation of the standard bell pattern.

IBO SHAKER RHYTHM

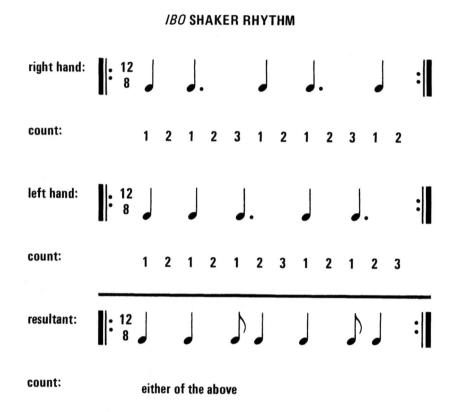

The obvious method of counting the resultant is to count it 1 2 1 2 1 1 2 1 2 1 1 2, but it can also be counted by using the counts for either the right-hand or the left-hand part.

---

[10]L. Ekweme, *Ibo Choral Music—Its Theory and Practice*, (Yale University Ph. D., 1972).

2. The following exercises were adapted from transcriptions of music of the *Eve* tribe made by the noted African music scholar, A.M. Jones.[11] The *Eve* people often use nonsense syllables to remember a resultant rhythm. Here, the syllable *dzi* is used for the four hand claps, and the syllable *GO* is used for the bell.[12] Where both parts coincide, the syllable is that of the clap. The *Eve* think of the resultant rhythm as *ending* on the first beat of the bell and therefore starting in the second note of the bell pattern. This brings up a principle in African music, which is the tendency for a second pattern to regard the first note of a background pattern as the place to end a phrase rather than to begin one. In both vocal and instrumental music, the African unifies his time with the last beat he plays rather than the first.

EVE BELL PATTERN

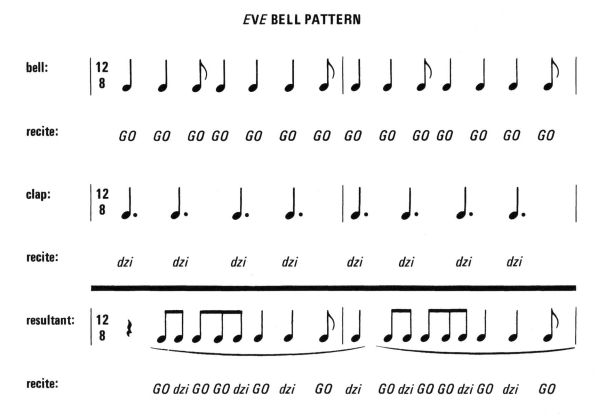

[11]A.M. Jones, *Studies in African Music*, (London: Oxford University Press, 1959), I, 53.

[12]A pronunciation guide to *Eve* drum syllables is included at the end of this chapter.

3. The notes of the *Kagan* (a small barrel drum) are represented by a set of nonsense syllables that includes the drum's name. Recite the *Kagan* part while clapping or playing the bell part to get a feel for the texture of the two parts together.

BELL PATTERN WITH *KAGAN*

4. In this exercise, the *Kagan* plays phrases of groups of four against the bell pattern.

*KAGA*N PHRASED IN FOUR

bell:

recite: GO   GO   GO GO   GO   GO   GO

*kaga*n:

recite: ka ga gan   ka ga gan   ka ga gan

resultant:

recite: GO ka ga gan GO ka ga gan   ka ga gan

5. This exercise shows the relationship between the bell part and the *axatse* (a gourd rattle with a bead net) part in *Eve takada* dance drumming. Here the syllable *GO* is used for the bell and the sound *ts* for the *axatse*. Recite the *axatse* part while clapping or playing the bell part to get a feel for the texture of the two parts together.

BELL PATTERN WITH *AXATSE*

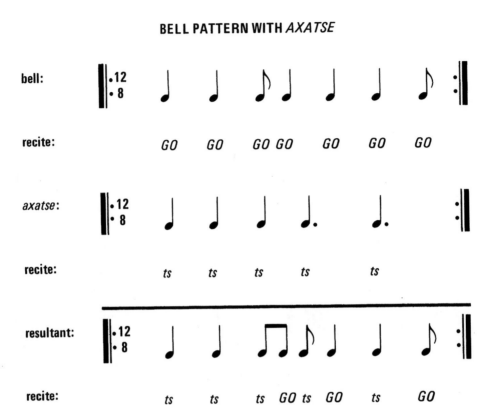

EXERCISE VI

Partners

Divide the parts of Exercises II through V between two or more partners. Try playing the parts on instruments such as drums, rattles and bells.

EXERCISE VII

Eve **Drum Music**

The following exercises were adapted from actual examples of *Eve* drum music. They are designed as group exercises in African ensemble rhythm. The first exercise, *Sovu*, was adapted from a transcription by A.M. Jones from his ground-breaking work, *Studies in African Music*.[13] The second, *Takada* Drumming, was adapted from a transcription by S. Kobla Ladzekpo and Hewitt Pantaleoni, who have developed a new notational system for African rhythms.[14]

The exercises can be performed utilizing traditional African instruments, commonly available substitutes, or by clapping and reciting the parts out loud. A chart of traditional *Eve* instruments (with suggested substitutes) is included at the end of this chapter.

Once the ensemble has mastered the exercises, experiment with allowing the *atsimevu* and *kidi* to improvise variations of their parts.

[13]A.M. Jones, *Studies in African Music*, (London: Oxford University Press, 1959), II, 77-79.

[14]S. Kobla Ladzekpo and Hewitt Pantaleoni, "*Takada* Drumming," *African Music, Journal of the African Music Society*, vol. 4, no. 4, 6-31.

SOVU

Among the *Eve* people of Ghana, there exist a number of religious cults. The *Yeve* cult is the "Cult of the God of Thunder", a secret society in which all members must be initiated by learning the special cult language, songs, dances and customs. *Sovu* is one of the cult dances which can be performed at any time when the members meet.

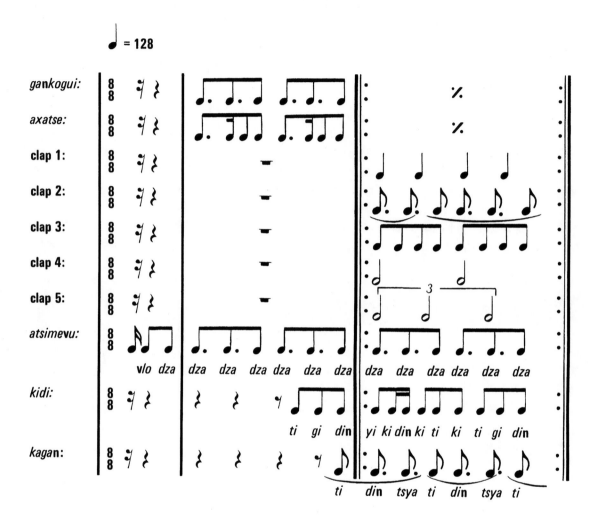

B.   *TAKADA* DRUMMING

The *Eve* people of the island town of *Anyako* off the coast of Southeastern Ghana cultivate a style of dance drumming known as *takada* drumming. An afternoon or evening of *takada* music begins with invocational drumming and singing to the gods followed by vigorous dancing accompanied by the full ensemble. Then comes an interlude movement of leisurely singing of club songs to the accompaniment of bells. This is then followed by vigorous dancing started with a song. A portion of the full ensemble dance music is presented here.

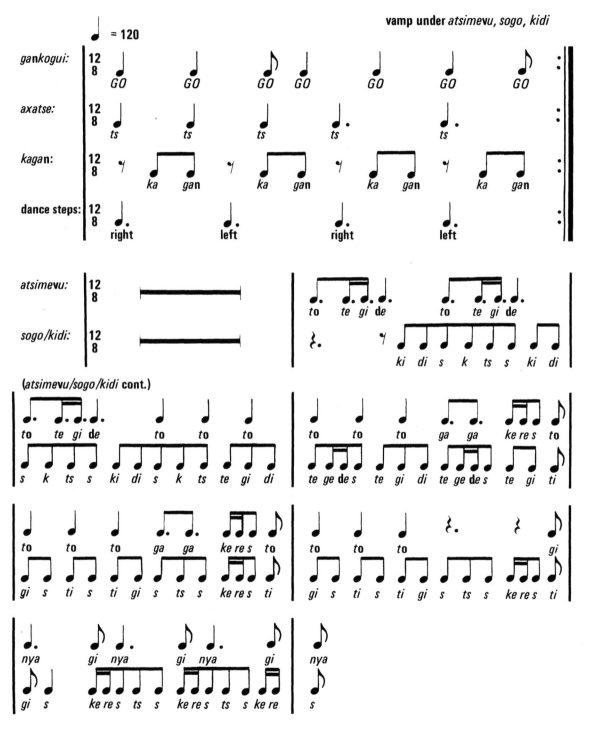

EVE INSTRUMENTS

NAME	CHARACTERISTICS	FUNCTION	SUBSTITUTE
Atsimevu	A large drum about five feet in length. Open at the bottom, it is sometimes carved from the trunk of a tree, but more often is of the barrel type. It is played with either a stick in both hands or with one stick and one bare hand. It is the lowest pitched drum in the *Eve* orchestra.	Leads the ensemble, provides the cues for changing patterns, is responsible for integrating well with the dancers and social situation, and makes improvised variations.	large conga, tumbadora, or any large barrel drum
Axatse	A rattle made of a calabash gourd with a bead net, played by hitting it downwards on to the thigh or upwards against the left hand while holding it in the right hand.	Provides background rhythm for the ensemble. The rattle patterns are coterminus with and derived from the pattern of the *gankogui*, but are not usually identical.	any rattle
Gankogui	A forged iron double bell played with a metal rod.	Provides the unifying rhythm which keeps the whole orchestra in time.	gong-gong, agogo, or any double bell
Kagan	A small narrow drum of the barrel variety. It is the highest in pitch of all of the drums in the *Eve* orchestra. It is open at the bottom and therefore is tipped up to let the vibrations out. The player grips it with his knees while sitting at a stool. It is played with two sticks.	Provides a supportive and stabilizing role in the ensemble.	any small narrow drum with an open bottom.
Kidi	A medium-sized barrel drum with a closed wooden bottom. It is slightly smaller and higher in pitch than the *sogo*. It is played with two sticks and is the second-highest pitched drum in the *Eve* orchestra.	Plays in rhythmic unison with the *sogo*, and responds to the patterns of the *atsimevu* with complimentary figures.	small conga or other medium-sized barrel drum
Sogo	A medium-sized barrel drum with a closed wooden bottom. It is slightly lower in pitch than the *kidi*, and is the second-lowest pitched drum in the orchestra. It is played with two sticks, two bare hands, or a combination of one stick and one bare hand.	Plays in rhythmic unison with the *kidi*, and responds to the patterns of the *atsimevu* with complimentary figures.	small conga or other medium-sized barrel drum

EVE TRANSLITERATION

The *Eve* alphabet contains letters that are not in the Roman system. These sounds are represented in this work by not italicizing certain letters. The following chart is given as a guide to *Eve* pronunciation.

Symbol	Sound
D *or* d	sounded by the tip of the tongue against the roof of the mouth
O *or* o	the vowel sound AW
N *or* n	the English NG
V *or* v	a V done with the lips rather than the lower lip and upper teeth
E or e	ranges in sound from UH to EH to AY as in SAY
S or s	a sound between SH and a hiss
X *or* x	the guttural CH of the Scottish LOCH
TS or ts	the English CH
DZ or dz	the English J

GLOSSARY OF *EVE* TERMS

atsimevu: a long, large barrel drum.

axatse: a rattle made of a calabash gourd with a bead net.

gankogui: a forged iron double bell.

kagan: a small, narrow drum of the barrel variety.

kidi: a medium-sized barrel drum.

sogo: a medium-sized barrel drum.

sovu: cult dance of *Eve* people.

takada: an *Eve* dance drumming style.

yeve: *Eve* "Cult of the God of Thunder."

GLOSSARY OF WESTERN MUSICAL TERMS USED TO DESCRIBE AFRICAN RHYTHM

additive rhythm: the use of groupings of different numbers of small-increment pulses to add up to the rhythmic phrase, generally forming an asymmetrical pulse combination. For example, pulse groupings of $2 + 3 + 2 + 2 + 3$ may be used to add up to a phrase of 12 pulses.

bi-rhythm: two different meters played simultaneously. Commonly used bi-rhythms in African music include two against three, three against four and three against eight.

cross rhythm: the juxtaposition of additive and divisive rhythms; also juxtaposition of two different divisive rhythms.

divisive rhythm: the division of a time span into equal pulses.

duple meter: the division of a time span into a group of two, four, eight, or sixteen (etc.) equal pulses.

hemiola: the use of alternating sections of duple and triple meter.

multiple meter: the simultaneous use of two or more meters.

resultant: the sound created when two interlocking parts are played together.

triple meter: the division of a time span into a group of three, six, twelve, or twenty-four (etc.) equal pulses.

time span: a fixed unit of time which can be broken up into either an equal number of segments, or pulse groupings of different time values. The time span is equal to the amount of time it takes for one cycle of the bell pattern to go by.

CHAPTER 2

BALI

Interlocking Parts

On the tropical island of Bali, music, art, dance and nature interweave with the fabric of village society. To the Balinese, art and music are inseparable from life itself. Art is not considered a luxury; it is a necessity. The social attitude towards art encourages a high level of involvement from a high percentage of the population. Nearly every rice farmer is also involved in the art of music, dance, painting, wood carving or sculpture. Artistic standards are high—a discrepancy of a fraction of a beat during a musical performance will evoke a rash of criticism among the audience. Artistic abilities are evident at a very young age, for the influence of the Balinese artistic attitude on the newborn is profound. Young children play music, paint and dance with a remarkable degree of proficiency. The women make daily offerings to the gods with rice and other foods, often so ornate and meticulously constructed as to become works of art in and of themselves. Music is performed for almost every religious occasion, of which there are many, for the Balinese are very devoted to their Hindu religion. Temple ceremonies, weddings, cremations, birthdays, tooth-filing ceremonies and scores of other auspicious occasions require musical accompaniment to please both gods and men.

Orchestras of tuned gongs, bronze kettles, bronze metallophones, bamboo xylophones, drums, cymbals and flutes fill the night air with animated music. These *gamelans* are the undertaking of a village club that includes not only the musicians but the dancers, costumers, singers, stage hands and benefactors as well. The music and dance interweave to form one entity, with the musicians taking cues from the dancers and vice versa.

The music is almost completely composed, with the exception of the drum part, which may contain improvisation. The composer does not notate the music, but rather, once the parts are set in his mind, teaches the music section by section to the members of the *gamelan*. All pieces are taught by rote, be they newly composed or from the traditional repertoire. The teacher shows each musician his part by playing it from the rear side of the instrument while the musician learns it from the front side. This allows the student to see where each note is played on his instrument and permits student-teacher eye contact as well. The teacher must play the part backwards to accomplish this, for normally the high notes are to the right, but from the rear the order is reversed. The teacher must know all of the parts for all of the instruments, and be able to play them both backwards and forwards.

Gamelan music is based on five tones, named *ding, dong, dèng, dung and dang*. These tones are spiritually linked with the gods of the five directions and their corresponding mystical colors. According to Hindu belief, in the center of a lotus sits *Batara Siva*, the Lord God of All and God of the Center Direction who is spiritually linked with the first tone, *ding*. The petals of the lotus in the following illustration show the relationships between the gods, directions, colors and tones.

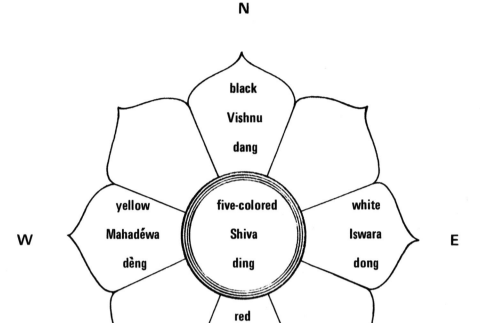

N

black
Vishnu
dang

yellow
Mahadéwa
dèng

five-colored
Shiva
ding

white
Iswara
dong

W

E

red
Brahma
dung

S

Two main tonal systems are used in Balinese music. *Sléndro* is a pentatonic scale of semi-equidistant intervals. The scale is very roughly equivalent to that produced by the black keys on the piano. *Pélog* is a seven-note tonal system from which a number of pentatonic modes are derived, the most common being known as *selisir*. The terms *pélog* and *sléndro* are borrowed from Javanese music, which shares common origins with Balinese music. While seven-note *pélog* is in common use in Javanese music, in Balinese music the developmental emphasis has been quite concentrated on the pentatonic forms. Shown in the musical examples on the following page are pentatonic *pélog* and *sléndro* scales, as well as a four-tone *sléndro* mode derived from pentatonic *sléndro* by simply omitting the note *dong*.

BALINESE TONAL SYSTEMS
ROUGH WESTERN APPROXIMATIONS

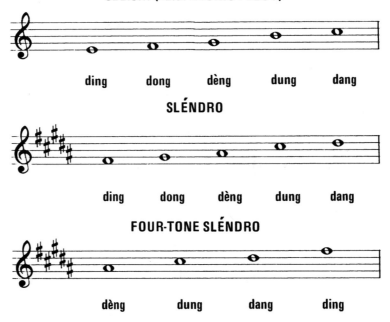

The tones in Balinese music do not fall within the confines of the 12-tone equal-tempered tuning system, as most of the notes fall in between the keys of the piano. The tunings of both *sléndro* and *pélog* vary considerably between *gamelans*, and during the author's stay in Bali, he found that the most intriguing *gamelans* were those with the more "jarring" tunings. At first exposure Westerners may find this quality somehow displeasing, but as cultural conditioning wears away, this same "jarring" quality becomes enchanting, intriguing and even sweet.

Gamelan instruments are tuned in matched pairs, characterized as male and female, with the male slightly higher in pitch than the female. The difference in tuning creates the shimmering effect that is so characteristic of Balinese music. "Vive la différence!"

Each instrument in the *gamelan* has its own function. Over the slow entrancing bass part played on large five-key metallophones, moves a basic melody known as *pokok* played on the *gendèr*, an instrument consisting of bronze keys suspended over bamboo resonators. When the Balinese notate their music for future reference, traditionally only the *pokok* tones are notated, for from these all else can be derived. Gongs of different sizes punctuate the music, marking different sections. The *gamelan* is usually led by the drummer, who gives the cues, controls the tempo and at times adds excitement by beating in torrents of cross rhythms. The *kajar*, a bronze kettle struck with a wooden mallet on each beat, keeps the meter steady. For emphasis, the music is punctuated by *angsels*, rhythmic accents performed in rhythmic unison by the drums, cymbals, metallophones and small bronze gongs with raised bosses. Often there are two drummers performing interlocking parts, at times hitting their drums simultaneously, but more often striking during each other's rests. High-pitched bronze metallophones ring out above, sounding like a legion of miniature hammers striking crystal keys. Here, too, the parts interlock, divided in such a way that musicians play alternate notes to form the melody line.

These interlocking parts, known as *kotèkans*, require cooperation and a keen sense of rhythm to perform. Not only must the musician perform his own part correctly, but he must be aware of the other musician's part and how it fits together with his to form the melody. The two parts of a *kotèkan*, which are thought of as male and female, are known as *nyangsih* and *polos*. The main accents of the *nyangsih* part are usually on the offbeat, while the main accents of the *polos* part are usually on the beat.

The concept of *kotèkan* is a part of Balinese life. Women husk rice by hitting the grains with poles in alternation, creating *kotèkans* and adding interest to worldly tasks. *Kotèkans* are also found in the natural environment. The mating calls of rice paddy frogs are remarkably like *kotèkans*, and may have had an influence in their development. Even now, in the village of Pliatan, the *gamelan gènggong* performs music directly imitating the sound of frog calls.

Kotèkans require a certain relaxed awareness to perform. It is often unexpectedly difficult for many Western musicians to perform *kotèkans*, for not being accustomed to the type of listening necessary, many lose the beat when first hearing the other part. This is in stark contrast to the Balinese, who often have trouble playing the *nyangsih* without the *polos*. The Balinese memorize the resultant melody created by the two parts of a *kotèkan*, and the *nyangsih* becomes automatic upon hearing the *polos*.

Knowledge and ability with *kotèkans* can be extremely valuable to those interested in creating new music. *Kotèkans* have a unique way of bringing people together in cooperation towards a common goal, and there are many creative possibilities for applying them to contemporary music.

KOTEKAN EXERCISES

The following exercises are designed as an introduction to *kotèkans*. They require one or more partners to perform, although in the absence of suitable partners much progress can be made by the individual musician through familiarization with the material. The exercises should ideally be performed on two of the same type of instrument, such as two percussion instruments, two violins, two flutes, two guitars, two voices or even two homemade instruments. For example, drinking glasses filled with different levels of water and struck with chopsticks make excellent instruments for performing *kotèkans*. The pitch need not be the exact pitch given here, as these are just rough Western approximations, although it is important that the relationships between high and low notes remain similar. The difference in pitch between homemade instruments and those given here will not change the effect of the *kotèkans* and may even lead one into an exploration of new tuning systems. One's imagination and the materials available are the only limitations.

It is recommended that both partners familiarize themselves with both the *nyangsih* and the *polos* before attempting to play a *kotèkan* together. The rhythms should also be tapped out on the thighs, the *polos* with one hand and the *nyangsih* with the other. It is also helpful to keep the beat with one hand while tapping the *nyangsih* or the *polos* with the other. When performing the *kotèkans* with a partner, the notes of one's part should sustain until the attack of the next note of the complementary part, then they may be stopped or dampened to allow the other part to be heard.

A NOTE ON NOTATION

The music in this chapter is written in Western notation with the *gong* stroke, which is the most heavily accented beat of the rhythmic cycle, as the first beat. The Balinese do not count the *gong* stroke as the first beat, but rather as the last, the beat after the *gong* stroke being the first beat. Since the *gong* stroke is similar in concept to the Indian *sam* (see Chapter 3) and the Western down-beat, it makes more sense in terms of the accent patterns implied by Western notation to write the *gong* stroke on one. Practice counting the *gong* stroke as the last beat, as shown below.

The symbol "θ" is utilized in this work to indicate the *gong* stroke.

Unless otherwise notated, the *nyangsih* parts of a *kotèkan* are written as the top line, while the *polos* parts are written as the bottom line.

For technical reasons, a sixteenth rest is sometimes used in place of a tie in syncopated passages.

In order to allow both the parts of a *kotèkan* to be heard clearly, the eighth notes must be played as if they were sixteenth notes followed by sixteenth rests. Sixteenth notes are to be played with exact time values. The above example should sound as shown below:

EXERCISE I

Rice-Pounding Music[1]

Not very long ago, before modern rice mills were commonplace in Bali, pounding unhusked rice to remove the hulls was a daily task. Although the use of rice mills to remove the hulls has become the norm, the traditional method is still in use in remote areas. Two to four women stand around a long wooden trough filled with rice, pounding with long, heavy poles. The poles are dropped in regular alternation, and since the poles are not uniform, each pole has its own sound and pitch. When there is much rice to be husked, it is the custom for the boys and men to gather around the women and beat out a lively accompaniment known as a *chandetan* on the trough, thus turning work into play. The women's part is known as the *ngijengin*, which means the "stationary, unchanging part".

If possible, perform these exercises with one or more players for each part. If there are two participants, play each part against all of the other parts. Practice tapping each rhythm while keeping the beat with the other hand. To better understand how the parts interlock, tap the first rhythm with one hand and a second rhythm with the other.

A. *Ngijengin*, the rice-pounding part, is shown here for two or four participants.

1.
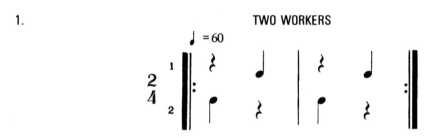
TWO WORKERS

2.
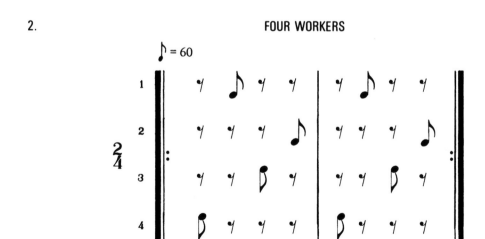
FOUR WORKERS

[1]From Colin McPhee, *Music in Bali*, (New Haven and London: Yale University Press, 1966), 359-362.

B. The *ngoplak* and *nyandet* parts are basic constituents of the *chandetan* accompaniment. The *nyandet* often occurs in two parts, although a second part is optional. The *nyandet* parts tend toward fixed, short, repeating patterns, while the *ngoplak* may extend into an independent improvised "solo".

If there are enough participants, play these exercises over the four-worker *ngijengin* part shown in Exercise I.A.2. Experiment with allowing the *ngoplak* player to improvise a "solo" using quarter notes, quarter rests, eighth notes and eighth rests.

C. A *kotèkan* is often played over the *nyandet* and the *ngoplak*. The two parts, *nyangsih* and *polos*, create an interplay that is double the speed of the *nyandet-ngoplak* interplay.

EXERCISE II

Kotèkan Cards

At the back of this book are three pages of cards. Cut them out and use them to get familiar with *kotèkan* rhythms. Each card represents one beat, the top rhythm being the *nyangsih* part and the bottom rhythm being the *polos*. There are 48 cards, with 26 different rhythms.

Assemble four- and eight-beat *kotèkan* rhythms. Tap out both the *nyangsih* and the *polos* parts. Be able to play both parts together, each part separately and each part with a partner playing the corresponding part.

After getting familiar with the *kotèkans* in Exercises III through V, compose melodies for four- and eight-beat *kotèkan* rhythms. It helps to start by using only two notes in each part. Where the two parts meet, pay consideration to how they harmonize.

There are four types of melodic *kotèkans* recognized in North Bali[2]. The *chandetan* is an alternating rhythm in which the *nyangsih* melody differs from the *polos*, while the *tutugan* is an alternating rhythm in which the *nyangsih* melody follows the *polos*. The *ochètan* is an interlocking rhythm in which two seperate voices are created where the parts meet, while the semi-*ochètan* is an interlocking rhythm in which the parts meet on a unison. The following examples were created using the *kotèkan*-card rhythms.

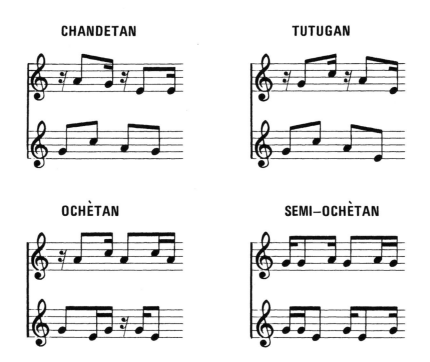

Using the *kotèkan*-card rhythms, create melodic *kotèkans* that exemplify each of the four types of figuration. Once a thorough understanding of how *kotèkans* work is acquired, experiment with integrating them into contemporary music.

[2]Colin McPhee, *Music in Bali*, (New Haven and London: Yale University Press 1966), 332.

EXERCISE III

These *kotèkans* are from the repertoire of the *gamelan anklung*, a four-tone *sléndro* ensemble that commonly accompanies temple ceremonies. The examples have been transposed to fall within the key of C to enable easy reading on a wide variety of instruments.

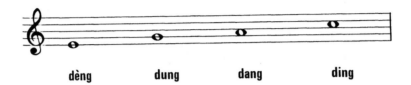

dèng   dung   dang   ding

D.

EXERCISE IV

Gendèr Wayang

The *gendèr wayang* is a five-tone *sléndro* ensemble of two sets of *gendèrs* (metallophones with bronze keys suspended over bamboo resonators), the second set doubling the first an octave above. The ensemble accompanies the *wayang*, the shadow play based on the Balinese versions of the Indian epics, the *Mahabharata* and the *Ramayana*.

The music for the shadow play is very well developed in its range of expressiveness and balance of form, and is highly evolved in its use of contrapuntal figuration. Each musician plays two distinct contrapuntal melodies using two mallets, one in each hand. The keys of the *gendèr* must be dampened so that long notes do not overlap. Because of this, the playing technique is difficult, as part of the hand must be used to dampen the last key played as the mallet simultaneously strikes the next key. The music is essentially four-voiced. Each musician plays a bass line and a melody line. At times, the two 2-voice parts interlock, forming a melodic *kotèkan* and an interlocking bass part. Often a single bass line is doubled, each musician playing the same bass line with the left hand while playing either the *nyangsih* or the *polos* part of a *kotèkan* with the right hand. In such cases, the exercises are written as three lines of music: the *nyangsih* right-hand part, the *polos* right-hand part, and the doubled left-hand bass line. The exercises can be rendered on two keyboards, two vibraphones, two classic guitars or two of any instrument capable of playing two voices at once. They can also be rendered by four single-voice instruments, or, in the exercises in which the bass line is doubled, three single-voice instruments. The exercises have been transposed to fall within the key of C, using the following Western approximation of the *sléndro* tuning system:

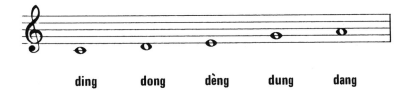

ding   dong   dèng   dung   dang

A.   PEMUNGKAH[3]

B.   PEMUNGKAH[4]

[3]This excerpt is from the conclusion of the opening section of a *pemungkah*, or opening music for the shadow play, composed by I Lotring for the Kuta village *gendèr wayang* quartet. From Colin McPhee, *Music in Bali*, (New Haven and London: Yale University Press, 1966), 207.

[4]This excerpt is from the interlude of a *pemungkah* composed by I Lotring for the Kuta village *gendèr wayang* quartet. From Colin McPhee, *Music in Bali*, (New Haven and London: Yale University Press, 1966), 214.

C.   ANGKAT-ANGKATAN[5]

EXERCISE V

The following *kotèkans* are from the repertoires of the *Gamelan Semar Pegulingan* and *gamelan gong kebyar*. All of the *kotèkans* are in the *selisir* mode of the *pélog* tuning system, and have been transposed to fall within the key of C.

ding   dong   dèng   dung   dang

[5]This excerpt is from the *angkat-angkatan*, a group of compositions played in shadow puppet performances during active scenes. From Colin McPhee, *Music in Bali*, (New Haven and London: Yale University Press, 1966), 383.

A. This basic *kotèkan* is prevalent in Balinese music.

B. This *kotèkan* is from the repertoire of the *Gamelan Semar Pegulingan*, the "*gamelan* of the Love God". The composition was taught to the author by I Madé Grindem in the village of Teges Kanyinan.

PÉRMAS

C. This excerpt is from *Tari Sesapi* (Swallow Dance), composed by I Komang Astita for *Gamelan Sekar Jaya*, a *gamelan gong kebyar* based in the San Francisco Bay Area. The piece was conceived in a modern form known as *kreasi baru* (new creation), based on traditional dance movements and music, yet incorporating new innovations as well.

TARI SESAPI

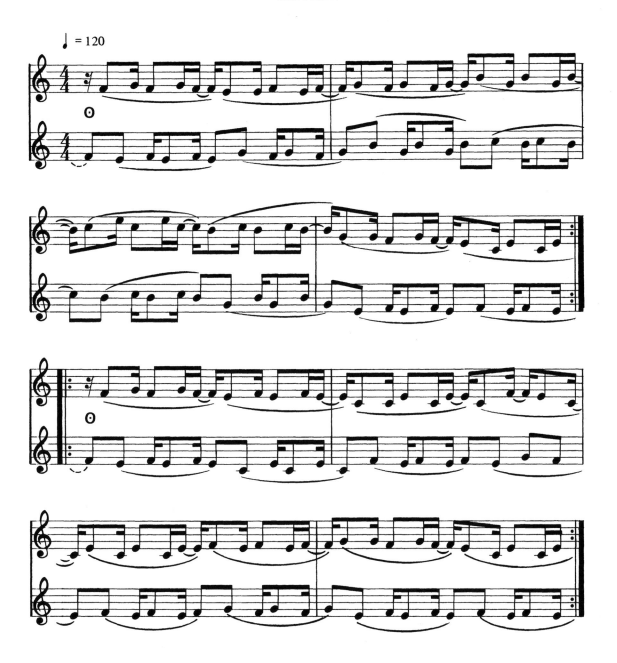

D. This *kotèkan* is from the composition *Léarsamas*, as performed in the village of Teges Kanyinan by the *Gamelan Semar Pegulingan*. Examine the way in which the *nyangsih* follows the *polos* in the first two bars.

LÉARSAMAS

E. *Gambangan* was created in 1926 by I Lotring, who is much admired by Balinese musicians for his innovations and his original music for the *gamelan pelègongan. Gambangan* is based melodically on two phrases of *Pelugon*, a composition from the repertoire of the *gamelan gambang*, and is a striking example of the way traditional material may be borrowed and modified to create a completely new piece of music. Lotring's use of melodic figuration represented an entirely new form of *kotèkan*, and consequently the composition created quite a sensation among Balinese musicians. While the *polos* follows the *pokok* tones in a simple rhythmic pattern of repeated tones, the *nyangsih* is highly syncopated, sounding almost entirely off the beat. One should not become discouraged if one has trouble synchronizing the *nyangsih* and *polos* at first, for this is undoubtedly the most difficult *kotèkan* presented in this work.

The composition is presented here as it is performed, minus the introduction and the coda, on the album "*Gamelan Semar Pegulingan*" (Nonesuch H-72046), recorded in Bali by Robert E. Brown.

GAMBANGAN

D. C. al Coda

GLOSSARY

angkat-angkatan: a group of compositions performed during the active scenes of the shadow puppet play.

angklung: an archaic form of tuned bamboo rattle from which the bronze-keyed *gamelan angklung* derives its name.

angsel: a rhythmic break in the music and dance movement.

batèl: rhythmic percussion accompaniment to stage scenes of battle.

chandetan: percussion accompaniment in rice-pounding music; one of four types of *kotèkan* recognized in North Bali, in which the parts alternate, the *nyangsih* melody differing from the *polos*.

dang: the fifth tone in the Balinese solfeggio system.

dèng: the third tone in the Balinese solfeggio system.

ding: the first tone in the Balinese solfeggio system.

dong: the second tone in the Balinese solfeggio system.

dung: the fourth tone in the Balinese solfeggio system.

gambang: a special form of bamboo xylophone retained from the past for the performance of cremation rites.

gambangan: a modern form of composition based on traditional *gambang* melodies.

gamelan: any ensemble composed primarily of percussion.

gamelan angklung: a four-tone *sléndro* ensemble that performs primarily at temple ceremonies.

gamelan gambang: an ensemble of bamboo xylophones that performs sacred music for cremation rites.

gamelan gènggong: an ensemble of wooden jaw harps.

gamelan gong gedé: a large five-tone *pélog* ensemble that was the forerunner of the *gamelan gong kebyar*.

gamelan gong kebyar: a modern ensemble developed in North Bali during the early part of the twentieth century, performing a contemporary repertoire of instrumental music for entertainment and festivity.

gamelan pelègongan: a five tone *pélog* ensemble that accompanies the *lègong* dance.

Gamelan Semar Pegulingan: a five or seven-tone ensemble named after the Love God.

gangsa: a metallophone with keys resting over a sound-box.

gedé: large; deep in pitch.

gendèr: a metallophone having a two-octave or wider range, with bronze keys suspended over tubular resonators.

gendèr wayang: the special *sléndro gendèr* used for the shadow play.

gending: instrumental composition.

gènggong: Balinese form of jaw harp, made from sugar palm wood .

gong: the name of the large gong used in many *gamelan* ensembles.

gongan: complete melodic period, terminating with a *gong* stroke.

jōgèd: popular form of dance performed by a young girl.

kajar: a small gong with sunken boss, used to keep the tempo steady.

kebyar: a modern dance, performed by a boy or young man to the *gamelan gong kebyar*.

kōtèkan: interlocking two-part figuration; in Java, the name for rice-pounding music.

kreasi baru: literally "new creation", this style of music and choreography developed in the 1960's is based on traditional music and dance but allows for the individual innovations of the choreographer and composer.

lagu: melody.

lègong: a form of dance performed by three small girls.

ngijengin: stationary, unchanging rice-pounding part.

ngōplak: constituent stroke of *chandetan* rice-pounding accompaniment.

nyandet: constituent stroke of *chandetan* rice-pounding accompaniment that tends towards fixed, repeating, syncopated parts.

nyangsih: (*sangsih*) differing; the generally offbeat part of a two-part *kotèkan* figuration.

ochètan: one of four types of *kotèkans* recognized in North Bali, in which the parts interlock and two seperate voices are created when the parts meet.

pélog: a seven-note scale system from which a number of five-tone modes are derived.

pemungkah: opening music for the shadow play.

pōkok: the basic, or nuclear, tones of a composition.

pōlos: (*mōlos*) simple, direct; the part of a *kotèkan* that follows the basic melodic line most closely, its main accents usually falling on the beat.

réong: a set of small gongs with raised bosses.

selisir: the most common five-tone scale derived from the seven-tone *pélog* scale.

sléndrō: a scale of semi-equidistant intervals, roughly equivalent to the black keys on the piano.

tabuh gari: closing music.

tari: dance.

tutugan: one of four types of *kotèkans* recognized in North Bali, in which the parts alternate, the *nyangsih* melody following the *polos*, repeating the same tones.

wayang: play

PRONUNCIATION GUIDE

a as in *bath*
final *a* as in *America*
e as in *the*
é as in *bay*
è as in *bet*
i as in *bin*
final *i* as in *tree*
o as in *dog*
ō (and final *o*) as in *so*
u as in *boot*
èr as in *air*
ge as in *gun*
ng as in *ing-o-plak*
ny as in *ni-yang-sih*

CHAPTER 3

INDIA

Rhythmic Cycles

The concept of the ever-recurring cyclic rhythms of the universe is one of the basic tenets of Hindu philosophy. The perception of the cyclic nature of life is reflected in Indian classical music through the device of *tala*, a recurring time-measure or rhythmic cycle. Just as in the Hindu religion, man is born, lives his life, dies and is then reincarnated to begin a new life, so the *tala* cycle begins, develops and then returns to the *sam*, the first beat of the cycle, anchor of all melody and rhythm and the leading beat to which all returns.

To master musicians of India, keeping track of *tala* is second nature. Through practice, Indian musicians develop an inner clock that keeps track of each beat of the *tala* while they improvise incredible cross-rhythmic variations against the rhythmic cycle. It is towards the development of this refined awareness of *tala* that the exercises in this section are presented.

There are two different traditions in Indian classical music, the *Carnatic* music of South India and the *Hindustani* music of North India. Both are oral traditions, handed down through the centuries from guru to disciple. The music of South India retained a purity of development that has led to a highly organized theoretical system, and for this reason this work will start by introducing the *Carnatic* rhythmic system.

RHYTHMIC CYCLES OF SOUTH INDIA

There exist several systems of cyclic organization of rhythm in use in South India, including the classical system of 108 *talas* and the later, more mathematically organized system of 35 *talas*. This work will cover the rudiments of the 35 *tala* system, which is now in common use. The *Carnatic* system breaks down rhythm into a complex set of components. To understand the system, the components that comprise South Indian rhythm must first be defined.

A *tala* is comprised of a number of beats, each of which is expressed by a gesture of the hands, of which there are three basic types. A beat may be expressed by an audible clap performed by clapping the right hand against the upturned palm of the left hand; it may be expressed by a silent wave of the hand performed by moving the right hand through an arc from the upturned palm of the left hand, stopping abruptly when the right-hand palm is level with the left-hand palm; or it may be expressed by silent finger movements performed by touching one finger of the right hand to the upturned palm of the left hand per beat to be counted, starting with the pinkie and proceeding through the other fingers to the number of beats necessary.

There are three basic components that combine to form a *tala*: the *anudrutam*, *drutam*, and *laghu*. The *anudrutam* is expressed by a hand clap and is always one beat in duration. It is represented by the symbol "**U**". The *drutam* is expressed by a hand clap followed by a hand wave. It is represented by the symbol "**O**" and is always two beats in duration. The *laghu* is the only component which is variable in its number of beats. It is expressed by one hand clap followed by two more finger counts. It is represented by the symbol "**I**". As *laghu* is variable in its number of beats, a number is often placed after its symbol to denote its duration. For example, **I**3 would be a *laghu* that is three beats in duration.

Jati refers to the number of beats in a *laghu*. *Jati* is variable through the five numerical groups shown below:

# BEATS PER LAGHU	JATI NAME
3	tisra jati
4	chaturasra jati
5	khanda jati
7	misra jati
9	sankirna jati

Thus the number of beats in a *laghu* may be three, four, five, seven or nine. Within any given *tala*, all *laghus* are the same number of beats in duration. There are seven principal *talas* in the 35 *tala* system, each an arrangement of one or more of the basic components of *tala*—*anudrutam*, *drutam* and *laghu*.

TALA NAME	COMPONENTS
dhruva	laghu, drutam, laghu, laghu
matya	laghu, drutam, laghu
rupaka	drutam, laghu
jhampa	laghu, anudrutam, drutam
triputa	laghu, drutam, drutam
ata	laghu, laghu, drutam, drutam
eka	laghu

Because *laghu* is variable in its number of beats through the five *jatis*, five separate *talas* are derived from each of the seven principal *talas* by simply changing the *jati*, producing 35 *talas*.

THE SCHEME OF THE 35 TALAS

7 PRINCIPAL TALAS	#	JATI VARIETY	# BEATS PER LAGHU	TALA NAME	SYMBOLIC REPRESENTATION	TOTAL # BEATS PER CYCLE
I. Dhruva	1	Tisra	3	Mani	I_3 O I_3 I_3	3 + 2 + 3 + 3 = 11
	2	Chaturasra	4	Srikara	I_4 O I_4 I_4	4 + 2 + 4 + 4 = 14
	3	Khanda	5	Pramana	I_5 O I_5 I_5	5 + 2 + 5 + 5 = 17
	4	Misra	7	Purna	I_7 O I_7 I_7	7 + 2 + 7 + 7 = 23
	5	Sankirna	9	Bhuvana	I_9 O I_9 I_9	9 + 2 + 9 + 9 = 29
II. Matya	6	Tisra	3	Sara	I_3 O I_3	3 + 2 + 3 = 8
	7	Chaturasra	4	Sama	I_4 O I_4	4 + 2 + 4 = 10
	8	Khanda	5	Udaya	I_5 O I_5	5 + 2 + 5 = 12
	9	Misra	7	Udirna	I_7 O I_7	7 + 2 + 7 = 16
	10	Sankirna	9	Rava	I_9 O I_9	9 + 2 + 9 = 20
III. Rupaka	11	Tisra	3	Chakra	O I_3	2 + 3 = 5
	12	Chaturasra	4	Patti	O I_4	2 + 4 = 6
	13	Khanda	5	Raja	O I_5	2 + 5 = 7
	14	Misra	7	Kula	O I_7	2 + 7 = 9
	15	Sankirna	9	Bindu	O I_9	2 + 9 = 11
IV. Jhampa	16	Tisra	3	Kadamba	I_3 U O	3 + 1 + 2 = 6
	17	Chaturasra	4	Madhura	I_4 U O	4 + 1 + 2 = 7
	18	Khanda	5	Chana	I_5 U O	5 + 1 + 2 = 8
	19	Misra	7	Sura	I_7 U O	7 + 1 + 2 = 10
	20	Sankirna	9	Kara	I_9 U O	9 + 1 + 2 = 12
V. Triputa	21	Tisra	3	Sankha	I_3 O O	3 + 2 + 2 = 7
	22	Chaturasra	4	Adi	I_4 O O	4 + 2 + 2 = 8
	23	Khanda	5	Dushkara	I_5 O O	5 + 2 + 2 = 9
	24	Misra	7	Lila	I_7 O O	7 + 2 + 2 = 11
	25	Sankirna	9	Bhoga	I_9 O O	9 + 2 + 2 = 13
VI. Ata	26	Tisra	3	Gupta	I_3 I_3 O O	3 + 3 + 2 + 2 = 10
	27	Chaturasra	4	Lekha	I_4 I_4 O O	4 + 4 + 2 + 2 = 12
	28	Khanda	5	Vidala	I_5 I_5 O O	5 + 5 + 2 + 2 = 14
	29	Misra	7	Loya	I_7 I_7 O O	7 + 7 + 2 + 2 = 18
	30	Sankirna	9	Dhira	I_9 I_9 O O	9 + 9 + 2 + 2 = 22
VII. Eka	31	Tisra	3	Sudha	I_3	3 = 3
	32	Chaturasra	4	Mana	I_4	4 = 4
	33	Khanda	5	Rata	I_5	5 = 5
	34	Misra	7	Raga	I_7	7 = 7
	35	Sankirna	9	Vasu	I_9	9 = 9

A beat may be divided into smaller units, just as in Western music a quarter note may be divided into eighth notes, triplets, sixteenth notes, and so on. *Gati* refers to the number of divisions per beat, and is variable through the five numerical groups shown below:

# DIVISIONS PER BEAT	GATI NAME
3	tisra gati
4	chaturasra gati
5	khanda gati
7	misra gati
9	sankirna gati

Thus the number of divisions per beat may be three, four, five, seven or nine. In performance, the *gati* normally remains consistent until it has been thoroughly explored and a climax has been reached, and then a different *gati* may be explored. Within a *gati*, multiples of the number of divisions per beat may be used. For instance, in *tisra gati*, six or twelve divisions per beat may be utilized to add interest and excitement to the performance. If no *gati* is mentioned, it is assumed to be *chaturasra gati*, or four divisions per beat.

Laya is the tempo or speed of the *tala*. Three degrees of *laya* are recognized:

LAYA NAME	TEMPO
vilambita	slow
madhya	medium
druta	fast

After familiarization with the elements of *tala*, the following exercises are indispensable in mastering what is known as *layajnanam*, one's rhythmic sense.

EXERCISE I

Onomatopoetic syllables are used by Indian drummers to form a kind of drum language, and some of these syllables are commonly used by musicians to count divisions within the *tala*. Memorize the following syllables and their pronunciations. Recite each syllable group a number of times in succession, giving each syllable one beat duration.

SYLLABLES	NUMERICAL GROUP
ta ki ta	tisra (3)
ta ka di mi	chaturasra (4)
ta ka ta ki ta	khanda (5)
ta ki ta ta ka di mi	misra (7, or 3 + 4)
ta ka di mi ta ka ta ki ta	sankirna (9, or 4 + 5)

PRONUNCIATION

tā, as in *taught*
kī, as in *key*
ka, as in *cub*
di, as in *dinner*
mī, as in *me*
ta ki ta: *tā*, as in *taught*; *kī*, as in *key*; *ta*, as in *tub*

EXERCISE II

Learn to keep track of the following *talas* on the hands using claps, waves, and finger counting.

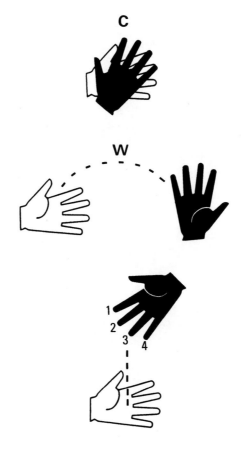

NOTATION

c = clap the right hand against the upturned palm of the left hand

w = wave performed by moving the right hand through an arc from the upturned palm of the left hand, stopping abruptly when the right-hand palm is level with the left-hand palm

1 = finger count performed by touching the first (index) finger of the right hand to the upturned palm of the left hand

2 = finger count performed by touching the second finger of the right hand to the upturned palm of the left hand

3 = finger count performed by touching the third finger of the right hand to the upturned palm of the left hand

4 = finger count performed by touching the fourth (pinkie) finger of the right hand to the upturned palm of the left hand

I_x = *laghu*, where x = # beats per *laghu*

O = *drutam*

U = *anudrutam*

A. CHATURASRA JATI TRIPUTA TALA (ADI TALA)—**I_4 O O** (8 BEATS)

tala **components** I_4 O O I_4

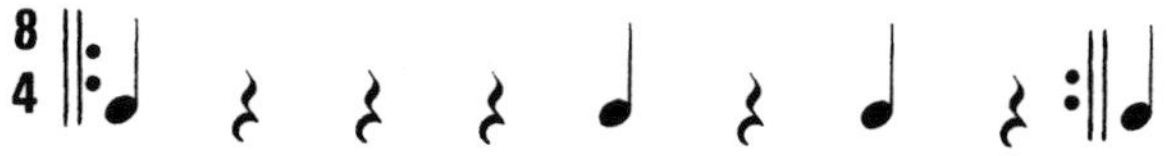

hand gestures C 4 3 2 C W C W C

B. KHANDA JATI JHAMPA TALA—**I_5 U O** (8 BEATS)

tala **components** I_5 U O I_5

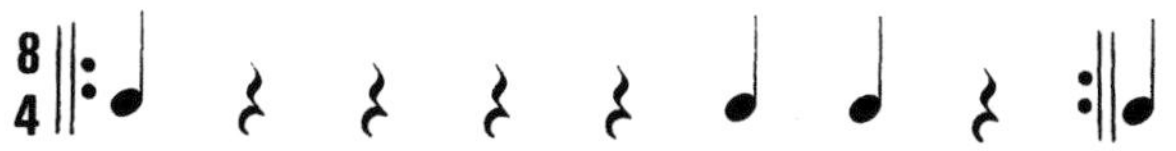

hand gestures C 4 3 2 1 C C W C

C. MISRA JATI EKA TALA—**I_7** (7 BEATS)

tala **components** I_7 I_7

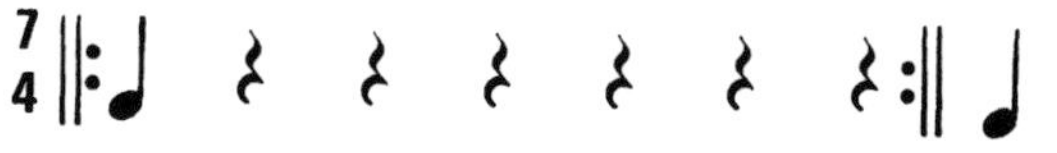

hand gestures C 4 3 2 1 4 3 C

D. TISRA JATI DHRUVA TALA—**I_3 O I_3 I_3** (11 BEATS)

tala **components** I_3 O I_3 I_3 I_3

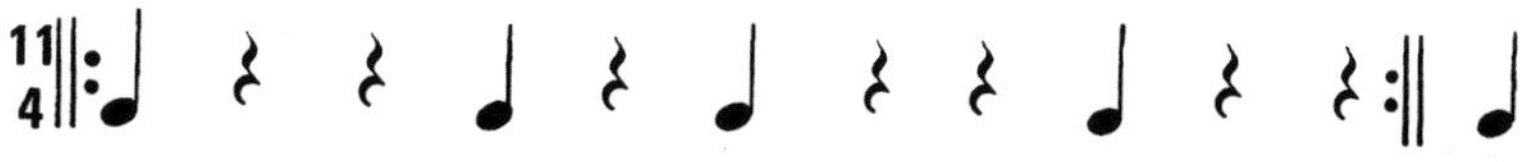

hand gestures C 4 3 C W C 4 3 C 4 3 C

EXERCISE III

This exercise divides each beat into smaller units, starting with three per beat (*tisra gati*) in Exercise A, and continues through the five *gatis* in Exercises B, C, D and E. The units are then phrased in groups of three's, four's, five's, seven's, and nine's. This exercise develops the ability to change phrase groupings in each of the five *gatis* while keeping the *tala*. Review this exercise periodically, as sections of it are advanced. It is one of the keys to mastery of *tala*. Here the exercise is presented in *adi tala (chaturasra jati triputa tala)*, but can be adapted to fit any *tala*.

A.   TISRA GATI

With three divisions per beat, one cycle of *adi tala* is 24 of these divisions long. Keep *tala* while reciting the syllables for the five numerical groups as shown below.

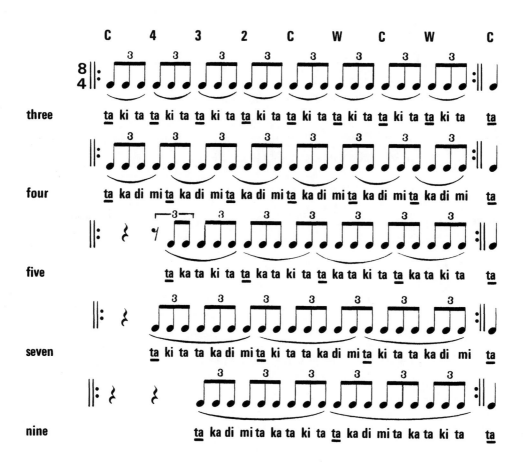

B.

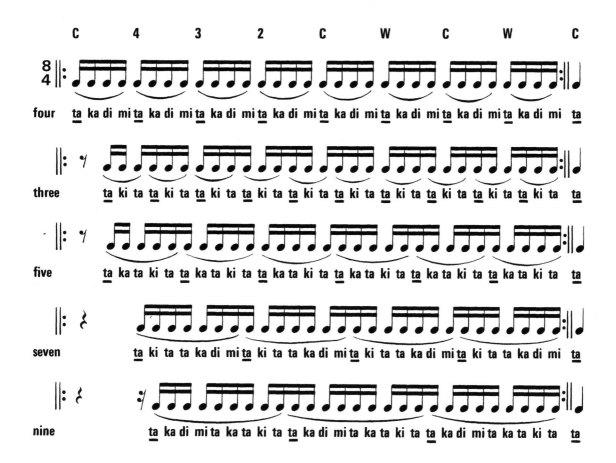

four   ta ka di mi ta ka di mi ta ka di mi ta ka di mi ta ka di mi ta ka di mi ta ka di mi ta

three   ta ki ta ta ki ta ta ki ta ta ki ta ta ki ta ta ki ta ta ki ta ta ki ta ta

five   ta ka ta ki ta ta ka ta ki ta ta ka ta ki ta ta ka ta ki ta ta ka ta ki ta ta

seven   ta ki ta ta ka di mi ta ki ta ta ka di mi ta ki ta ta ka di mi ta ki ta ta ka di mi ta

nine   ta ka di mi ta ka ta ki ta ta ka di mi ta ka ta ki ta ta ka di mi ta ka ta ki ta ta

C.

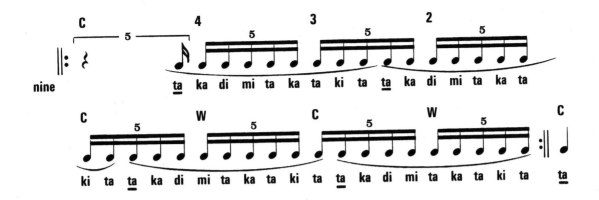

nine

ta ka di mi ta ka ta ki ta ta ka di mi ta ka ta

ki ta ta ka di mi ta ka ta ki ta ta ka di mi ta ka ta ki ta ta

D. MISRA GATI

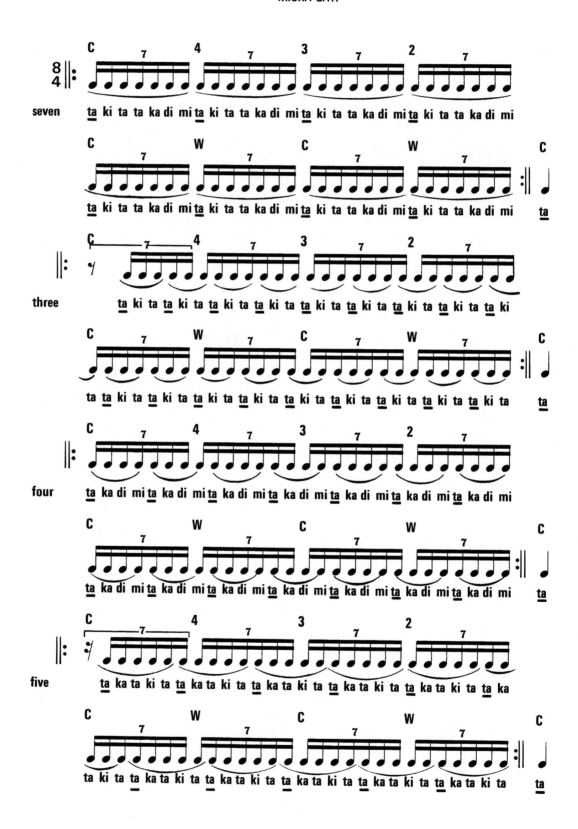

nine

ta <u>ta</u> ka di mi ta ka ta ki ta <u>ta</u> ka di mi ta ka ta ki ta <u>ta</u> ka di mi ta ka ta ki ta

<u>ta</u>

E.

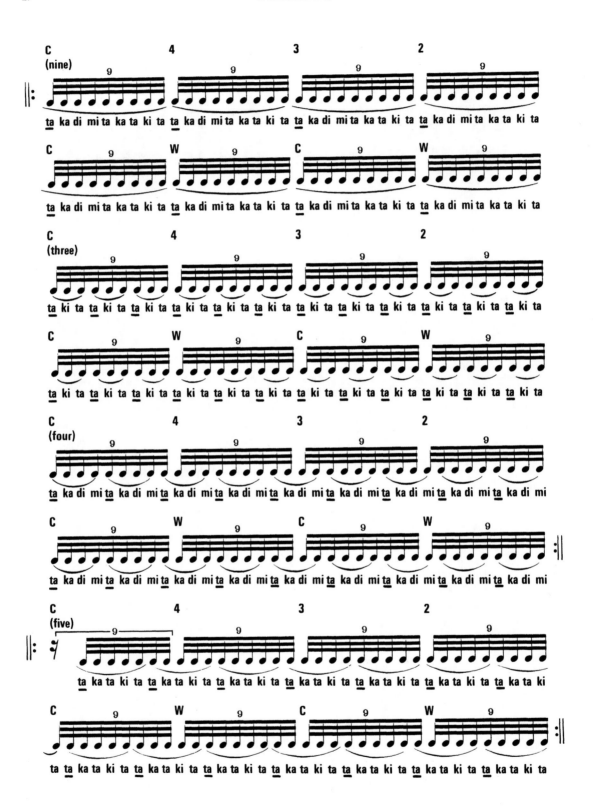

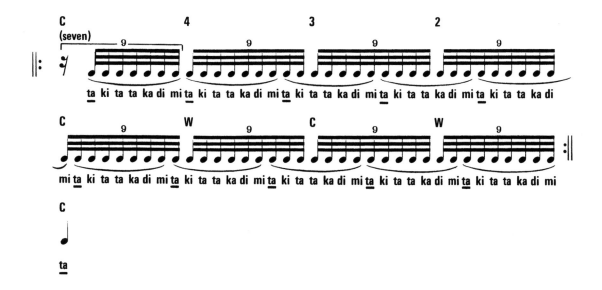

ta ki ta ta ka di mi ta ki ta ta ka di mi ta ki ta ta ka di mi ta ki ta ta ka di mi ta ki ta ta ka di

mi ta ki ta ta ka di mi ta ki ta ta ka di mi ta ki ta ta ka di mi ta ki ta ta ka di mi ta ki ta ta ka di mi

ta

EXERCISE IV

SOLKATTU

South Indian drumming has a language all of its own. For every sound produced by the *mridangam*, there is a corresponding syllable. These syllables, known as *solkattu*, are combined to form innumerable rhythms. The *solkattu* language becomes almost inseparable from the drumming itself.

The following *solkattu* composition excerpts were transcribed from studies with Guruvayoor Dorai, master of the *mridangam*, at the Center for World Music in San Francisco during the summer of 1978. They make an excellent exercise in rhythm, and are a thing of beauty in and of themselves. Keep the *tala* with the hands while reciting the *solkattu* compositions.

The compositions contain many *moras*, rhythmic phrases repeated three times, the final stroke culminating either on the *sam* or the starting point of the main phrase in a composition. Give special attention to each *mora*, as they are one of the unique rhythmic features of Indian music.

Before proceeding to the excerpts of compositions by Guruvayoor Dorai, get familiar with the basic syllables. The following is a list of those used in the compositions and an approximate guide to their pronunciation.

SYLLABLES	PRONUNCIATION
da	*ā*, as in *saw*
dim	*ī*, as in *key*
din	*i*, as in *pin*
dum	*ū*, as in *room*
gu	*ū*, as in *room*
ka	*a*, as in *up*
ki	*ī*, as in *key*
lan	*ā*, as in *saw*
na	*ā*, as in *saw*
ta	*ā*, as in *saw*
tam	*ā*, as in *saw*
tang	*ā*, as in *saw*
di mi	*i*, as in *pin*; *ī*, as in *key*
di na	*i*, as in *pin*; *ā*, as in *saw*
ju na	*u*, as in *put*; *ā*, as in *saw*
ki ta	*ī*, as in *key*; *a*, as in *up*
na ka	*ā*, as in *saw*; *a*, as in *up*
ta ka	*ā*, as in *saw*; *a*, as in *up*
ta ri	*ā*, as in *saw*; *ī*, as in *key*

ADI TALA (CHATURASRA JATI TRIPUTA TALA)

TISRA GATI

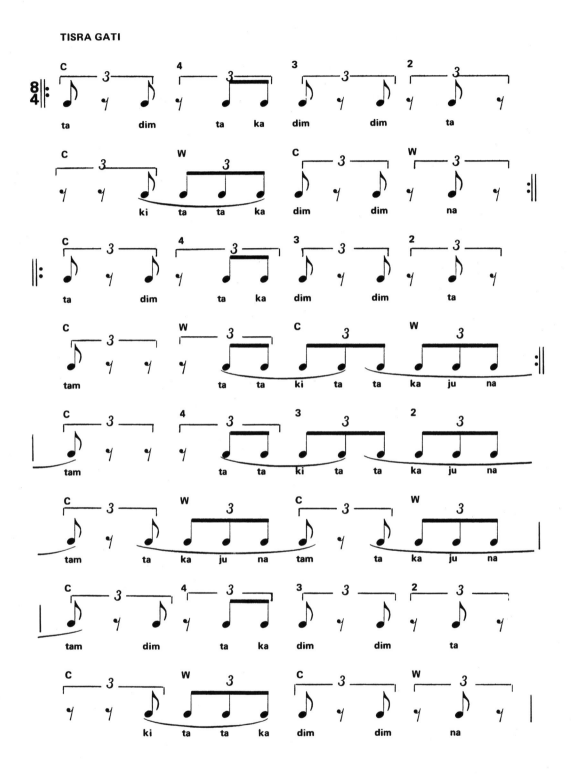

CHATURASRA GATI

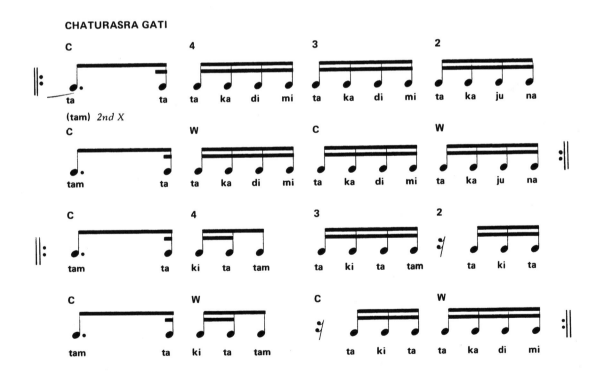

2nd X—insert **ding** in place of **dum**, 3rd X—insert **tang** and 4th X—insert **ta ri**.

3rd and 4th X of repeat—insert **ki ta ta ka ta ri ki ta tam** *in place of* **ta di ki ta tam.**

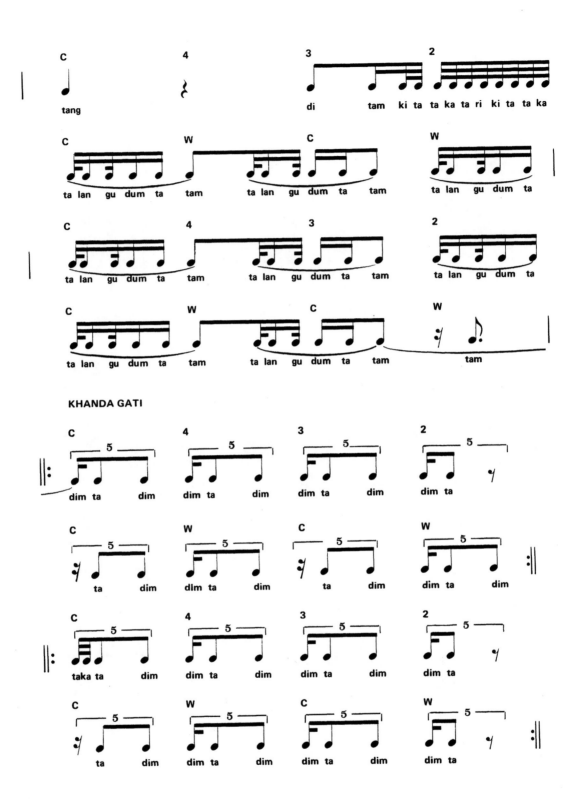

KHANDA GATI

87

GLOSSARY OF SOUTH INDIAN MUSICAL TERMS

ānudrūtam: one of the *tala* components, it is always one beat in duration and is expressed by a clap of the hands. Symbol-**U**.

āta tāla: the sixth of the seven principle *talas*, consisting of two *laghus* followed by two *drutams*. Symbol-**I I O O**.

Cārnātic music: the system of music prevailing in South India.

chātūrasra: an adjective signifying the numerical group four.

dhrūva tāla: the first of the seven principle *talas*, consisting of a *laghu* followed by a *drutam* and two *laghus*. Symbol-**I O I I**.

drūta lāya: fast tempo.

drūtam: one of the *tala* components, it is always two beats in duration and is expressed by a clap followed by a wave of the hands. Symbol-**O**.

ēka tāla: the seventh of the principle *talas*, consisting of a single *laghu*. Symbol-**I**.

gatī: literally "pace" or "movement", *gati* refers to the number of divisions per beat. It is the underlying rhythm of the *tala* and is variable through the five numerical groups.

jātī: literally "class", *jati* refers to the number of beats in a *laghu*, of which there are five classes.

jhāmpa tāla: the fourth of the seven principle *talas*, consisting of a *laghu* followed by an *anudrutam* and a *drutam*. Symbol-**I U O**.

khānda: literally, *khanda* means "broken". It signifies the numerical group five, which is often broken-down into 2 + 3.

lāghū: one of the *tala* components, it is variable in its number of beats through the five *jatis*, and is expressed in performance by a clap followed by a variable number of finger counts, depending on the *jati* used. Symbol-**I**.

lāya: speed or tempo of *tala*.

lāyajñānam: literally, *layajnanam* means "knowing time", i.e. sense of rhythm.

mādhya lāya: medium tempo.

mātya tāla: the second of the seven principle *talas*, consisting of a *laghu* followed by a *drutam* and a *laghu*. Symbol-**I O I**.

mīsra: literally, *misra* means "mixed". It signifies the numerical group of seven, which is divided into a group of three and a group of four.

mōra: a rhythmic phrase repeated three times, acting as a cadence which culminates either on the *sam* or starting point of a main phrase of the composition.

mridangam: a two-headed barrel drum made of jackwood with goat skin heads.

rūpaka tāla: the third of seven principle *talas*, consisting of a *drutam* followed by a *laghu*. Symbol-**O I**.

sam: the first beat of the *tala*.

sānkīrna: literally, *sankirna* means "composite". It signifies the numerical group nine, which is composed of a group of four and a group of five.

sōlkattū: the syllables of the *mridangam* drum language. Each syllable corresponds to a sound on the drum.

tāla: rhythmic cycle. Literally, "to beat the hands."

tīsra: an adjective signifying the numerical group three.

tripūta: the fifth of the seven principle *talas*, consisting of a *laghu* followed by two *drutams*. Symbol-**I O O**.

vilambīta lāya: slow tempo.

RHYTHMIC CYCLES OF NORTH INDIA

The luxuriance of *Hindustani* music is the result of a synthesis of Hindu and Muslim culture brought together by the Muslim invasions of North India. After the initial damage and devastation brought by the invasions and resulting clash of cultures subsided, a tremendous artistic flowering occurred, encouraged by the benevolent jurisdiction of rulers such as the Moghul Emperor Akbar, a Muslim who took a Hindu wife and inspired interaction between Hindu and Muslim cultures.[1] This renaissance led to a music rich in delicacy and diversity. Both *Hindustani* and *Carnatic* music can trace their roots back to the Vedas, but as South India was never physically touched by the Muslim invasions, *Carnatic* music has remained relatively uninfluenced by foreign cultures, producing a highly organized and developed rhythmic system. In contrast, *Hindustani* music has achieved its equally high artistic standards through the cultural interaction between Hindus and Muslims, producing an extremely rich but less-systemized music.

This process brought into being an estimated 350 *talas*, of which ten are most commonly used. Each cycle is a number of *matras*, or beats, in duration. *Matras* have different degrees of emphasis within a *tala*, and are marked with a system of hand claps, hand waves and movements of the fingers, much as *tala* is marked in South India. This marking of the beat using hand gestures is known as "keeping *tal*." The most important point of rhythmic emphasis is the *sam*, the first beat of the *tala* and point to which all variations eventually return. It is represented by the symbol "+." The *khali*, literally the "empty" beat, is the unaccented *matra* of the *tala*. The lack of accent is emphasized, making the *khali* a very important beat. It is marked by a wave of the hand and is written with the symbol "**o**." *Talas* have other accented beats known as *tali*, also marked by hand claps. They are not as heavily accented as the *sam*, but serve to divide the *tala* into smaller sections as do the *sam* and *khali*. In written notation, the *tali* are numbered, starting with the number two, as the *sam* is the first *tali*. For example, the *sam* is written "+," the second *tali* is written "**2**," the *khali* "**o**," the third *tali* "**3**," and so on.

The *tabla*, a two-piece drum with goat-skin heads, has a language all of its own. For every sound of the drum there is a corresponding syllable. These syllables are known as *bols*, and to the *tabla* master these onomatopoetic *bols* and their corresponding sounds on the drums are almost one and the same. *Tabla* players tend to think, eat, drink and sleep *bols*, often to the chagrin of their families, friends and fellow musicians.

Each *tala* has a *theka*, a standard set of *bols* that identify the *tala*. The *theka* aids the soloist in keeping *tal*. South Indian *talas* do not have *thekas*, so it is the function of both the melodic and rhythmic players to keep the *tal*, whereas in North Indian music the *tabla* player must keep the *tal* through the device of *theka*, although each musician must be able to keep *tal* in their minds, so as not to lose the rhythm when the *tabla* player does a particularly complex variation or improvisation.

Practice reciting the *thekas* on the following pages while keeping *tal*. The *thekas* of the ten common *talas* should be memorized, as well as any others one finds especially interesting. A pronunciation guide is included to aid in learning *bols*. Practice reciting each *theka* at a comfortable tempo.

[1] Peggy Holroyde, *The Music of India*, (New York: Praeger Publishers, 1972), 87.

TABLA BOLS

The following chart can be used in conjunction with the pronunciation guide at the end of this chapter to aid in the pronunciation of *tabla bols*. It should be noted, however, that India is a land of extreme linguistic variation, and there are many different pronunciations of these same *bols* in use in different regions.

BOLS	BOLS (cont.)
dē	re
dhā	ri
dhē	tā or ta
dhĭ	te
dhin	tet
dĭ	tin
din	trē
ga	tūn
gē	
gēn	**COMPOUND BOLS**
ka	
kat	ka ta
kē	kĭ ta
kĭ	tā ga
krē	tā gē
nā	tā kĭ ta

EXERCISE I

A.   TEN COMMON TALAS

1.   TINTAL- 16 MATRAS, DIVIDED 4 + 4 + 4 + 4

dha dhin dhin dha dha dhin dhin dha na tin tin ta ta dhin dhin dha dha

2.   SITARKHANI- 16 MATRAS, DIVIDED 4 + 4 + 4 + 4

dha ga dhi ge dha dha ga dhi ge dha dha ka ti ka ta ta ga dhi ge dha dha

3.   KEHARWA- 8 MATRAS, DIVIDED 4 + 4

dha ge na ti na ka dhi na dha

4.   DADRA- 6 MATRAS, DIVIDED 3 + 3

dhi dhi na dha tun na dhi

91

5. RUPAK- 7 MATRAS, DIVIDED 3 + 2 + 2

This *tala* is unusual in that both the *sam* and *khali* fall on the same beat. In keeping *tal*, use a wave and not a clap for the *sam/khali*.

6. JHAPTAL- 10 MATRAS, DIVIDED 2 + 3 + 2 + 3

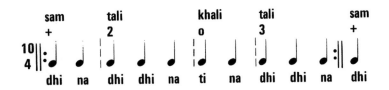

7. EKTAL- 12 MATRAS, DIVIDED 2 + 2 + 2 + 2 + 2 + 2

8.   CHACHAR- 14 MATRAS, DIVIDED 3 + 4 + 3 + 4

9.   CHOWTAL- 12 MATRAS, DIVIDED 2 + 2 + 2 + 2 + 2 + 2

10.   DHAMMAR- 14 MATRAS, DIVIDED 5 + 2 + 3 + 4

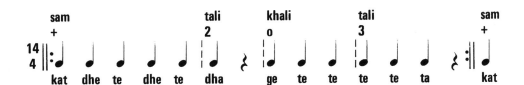

B.   FRACTIONAL TALAS

Fractional *talas* are expressed in terms of an integer and a fraction. They usually contain a grouping of 1½ beats at the end of the cycle.

1.   ARDHA JAITAL- 6½ MATRAS, DIVIDED 3 + 2 + 1½

Equivalent to a 13-*matra tala*, where each *matra* is ½ the time value.

93

2.   UPA DASI- 10½ MATRAS, DIVIDED 1½ + 1½ + 1½ + 1½ + 1½ + 1½ + 1½

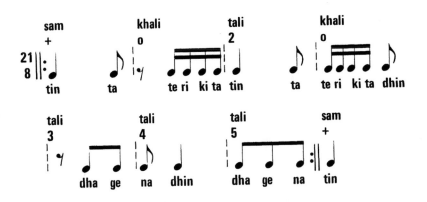

C.   SAWARI TALAS

Sawari talas contain two or more groupings of 1½ *matras*, causing an irregular rhythm pattern.

1.   CHARTAL KI SAWARI- 11 MATRAS, DIVIDED 2 + 2 + 2 + 2 + 1½ + 1½

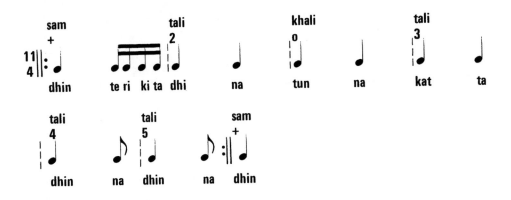

EXERCISE II

Laya

As in South India, *laya* refers to speed or tempo. There are three degrees of *tala* speed commonly recognized:

LAYA NAME	TEMPO
vilambit	slow
madhya	medium
drut	fast

In North India, *laya* also refers to the relative tempo against the *tala*. For example, if one is keeping *tintal* while playing three notes of equal time-value per beat, then the *laya* is said to be *tigun*, or three times the speed of the *tala*. The following is a chart of various degrees of relative tempo against the *tala*.

LAYA NAME	SPEED RELATIVE TO THE TALA
pao	¼
ardha	½
paun	¾
barabar	1
sawai	1¼
deri	1½
paune do	1¾
dugun	2
sawai do	2¼
arhai	2½
paune tin	2¾
tigun	3
sawai tin	3¼
sarhe tin	3½
paune char	3¾
chaugun	4
panchgun	5
chegun	6
satgun	7
atgun	8
nogun	9

The same syllables used in *Carnatic* music to count divisions within the *tala* can also be used in *laya* exercises.

SYLLABLES	NUMERICAL GROUP
ta	1
ta ka	2
ta ki ta	3
ta ka di mi	4
ta ka ta ki ta	5
ta ki ta ta ki ta	6
ta ki ta ta ka di mi	7
ta ka di mi ta ka di mi	8
ta ka di mi ta ka ta ki ta	9

The following is an exercise in changing *laya*, starting with one syllable per beat (*barabar laya*) and continuing through to nine syllables per beat (*nogun laya*). Keep slow *tintal* while reciting the syllables. Make sure that the tempo of the *tala* remains constant while changing the number of divisions per beat, starting with a tempo slow enough to recite the syllables used for *nogun laya*. Master each *laya* individually before attempting to perform the entire exercise.

BARABAR LAYA (1 X)

DUGUN LAYA (2 X)

TIGUN LAYA (3 X)

CHAUGUN LAYA (4 X)

PANCHGUN LAYA (5 X)

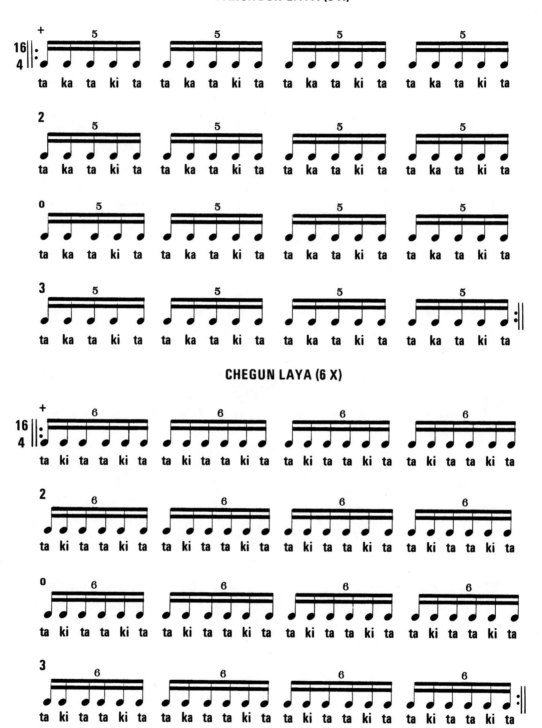

CHEGUN LAYA (6 X)

98

SATGUN LAYA (7 X)

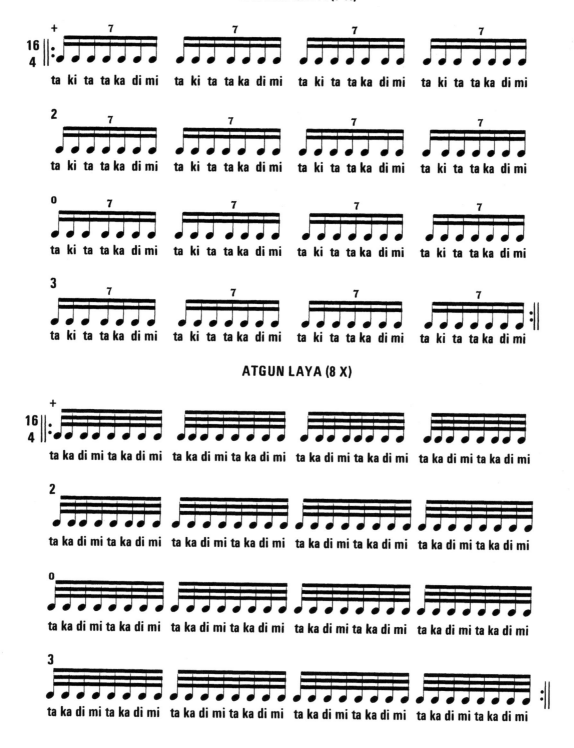

ATGUN LAYA (8 X)

NOGUN LAYA (9 X)

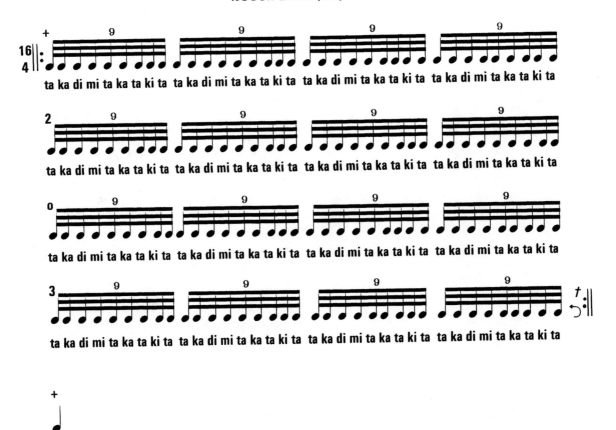

16/4 ta ka di mi ta ka ta ki ta ta ka di mi ta ka ta ki ta ta ka di mi ta ka ta ki ta ta ka di mi ta ka ta ki ta

2 ta ka di mi ta ka ta ki ta ta ka di mi ta ka ta ki ta ta ka di mi ta ka ta ki ta ta ka di mi ta ka ta ki ta

0 ta ka di mi ta ka ta ki ta ta ka di mi ta ka ta ki ta ta ka di mi ta ka ta ki ta ta ka di mi ta ka ta ki ta

3 ta ka di mi ta ka ta ki ta ta ka di mi ta ka ta ki ta ta ka di mi ta ka ta ki ta ta ka di mi ta ka ta ki ta

+

ta

† *Then proceed through the* **layas** *in reverse order, ending on* **sam** *after the final cycle of* **barabar laya.**

100

EXERCISE III

Chand

Chand refers to the way in which divisions within the *tala* are grouped or phrased. For example, within any *laya* the divisions of the beat can be grouped into one's, two's, three's, four's, five's and so forth. Within the grid of *laya* and *chand*, an amazing diversity of rhythmic accents is available for the reader's exploration. In improvisations by North Indian masters of rhythm, *laya* and *chand* are often changed suddenly to provide rhythmic excitement.

Use the following exercise to gain a thorough grasp of the concept of *chand*, and then apply this knowledge to the *layas* in Exercise II by grouping them in different *chand* patterns. Review Exercise III of the South Indian rhythm section of this book as it can also be conceived of as a *laya/chand* exercise. North Indian music uses the concept of *laya* to cover not only the tempo of the *tala*, but also to cover the same effect as the South Indian concept of *gati*, which is the pace of the movement of notes against the *tala*.

Keep *tal* while reciting the following syllables, phrasing them in the *chand* indicated. Make sure that the tempo stays constant throughout the exercise.

CHAND 1

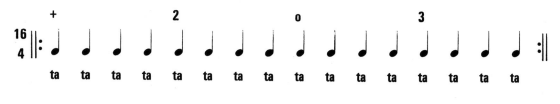

CHAND 2

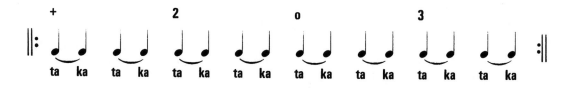

CHAND 3

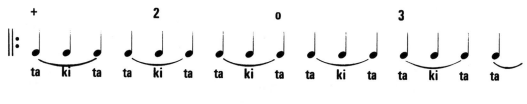

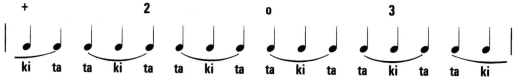

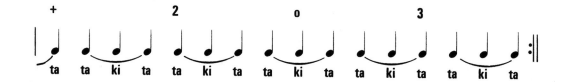

CHAND 4

CHAND 5

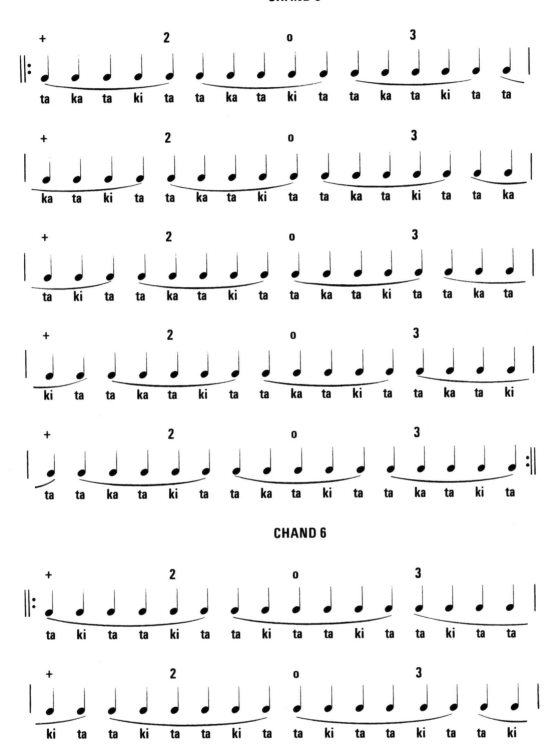

CHAND 6

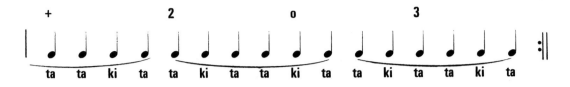

CHAND 7

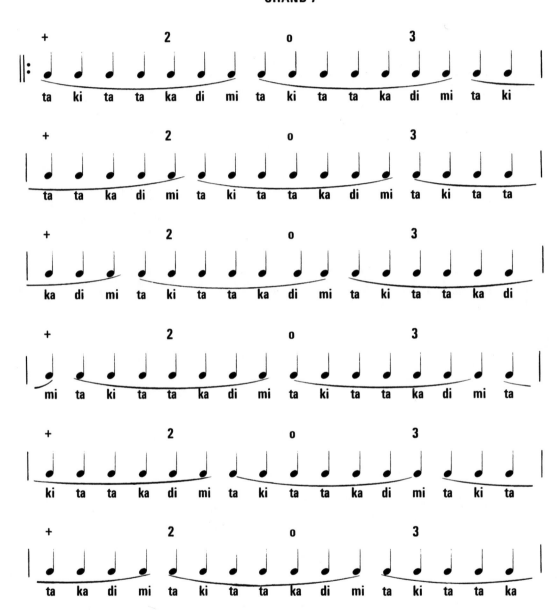

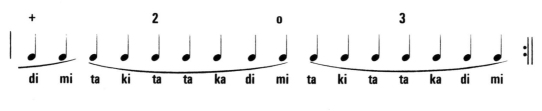

CHAND 8

CHAND 9

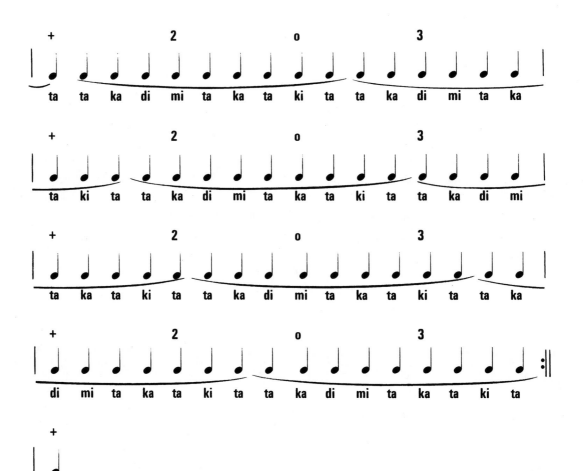

EXERCISE IV

Fractional Laya

The speed relative to the *tala* need not be limited to whole-number increments. Speeds such as 3¼ (*sawai tin laya*), 2¾ (*paune tin laya*) and 1½ (*deri laya*) are utilized by masters of *laya* (see chart at beginning of Exercise II).

In order to perform a fractional *laya*, one may first wish to look at its component parts. For instance, 1½ speed is three-halves faster than normal. To play at 1½ speed, one must play three notes where there were once two, or three against two. If one divides each beat of the original speed into three parts and groups these parts in two's, one ends up in *deri laya*, a speed 1½ times normal. One may utilize these principles to understand any fractional *laya*.

Practice alternating between *deri laya* and *tintal theka*. Notice that *deri laya* as written below could also be thought of as a *laya* of three grouped into two's (producing a *chund* of two). The resulting speed is 1½ times that of the *tala*, equivalent to "time and a half" in Western music.

DERI LAYA- 1½ SPEED

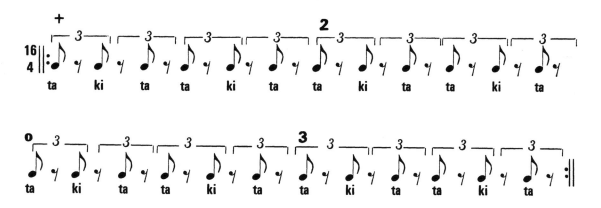

EXERCISE V

Accent Patterns

In four-count rhythmic figures, it is possible to put the accent on any one of the counts. The following is a chart of the possible accent positions and their Indian names.

BARABAR	SAWAI	ARI	KWARI
(equal)	(one-quarter after)	(one-half)	(three quarters after)
1̆ 2 3 4	1 2̆ 3 4	1 2 3̆ 4	1 2 3 4̆

The following exercise develops the ability to change the accent position while keeping *tintal*.

BARABAR   SAWAI   ARI   KWARI

ta ta ta ta   ta ta ta ta   ta ta ta ta   ta ta ta ta

EXERCISE VI

Tihais

A *tihai* is a cadential pattern repeated three times in succession. The last note of the cadence is timed to fall either on the *sam* or on the beginning note of a main musical phrase. One repetition of the pattern is known as a *pala*. Musicians become skilled at fashioning *tihais* on the spur of the moment to create a cadence, and must continually be aware of where they are in the rhythmic cycle and consequently how many counts are left in which to play a *tihai*. While North Indian musicians create *tihais* by a more or less intuitive process gained through years of practice and familiarization with the elements of *tala*, it is helpful to know mathematical formulas for arriving at *tihais*. A number of these formulas have been included here, and from these a multitude of *tihais* may be created.

A.   TIHAIS WITH GAPS

It is common for a gap or rest to be placed in between the *palas*. Recite the *bols* to the following *tihais* while keeping *tal*.

1.   MEDIUM FAST TINTAL

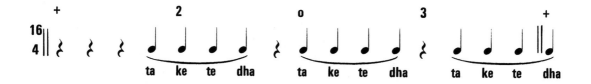

ta ke te dha   ta ke te dha   ta ke te dha

2.

MEDIUM RUPAK

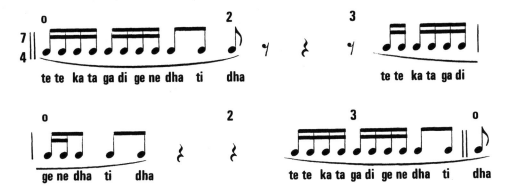

te te ka ta ga di ge ne dha ti dha   te te ka ta ga di

ge ne dha ti   dha   te te ka ta ga di ge ne dha ti   dha

3.

MEDIUM SLOW TINTAL

This *tihai* is based on a reduction pattern, starting with a nine-count phrase that is shortened by one count each time it is repeated, until it is only one count long. This entire composition is then repeated three times with a gap of five sixteenth notes between each *pala*.

te ri ki ta ta ka ta   te te ka ta ga di ge ne dha   ki ta ta ka ta   te te ka ta

ga di ge ne dha   ta ka ta   te te ka ta ga di ge ne dha   ta   te te

ka ta ga di ge ne dha   te te ka ta ga di ge ne dha   ka ta ga di ge ne

dha   ga di ge ne dha   ge ne dha   dha

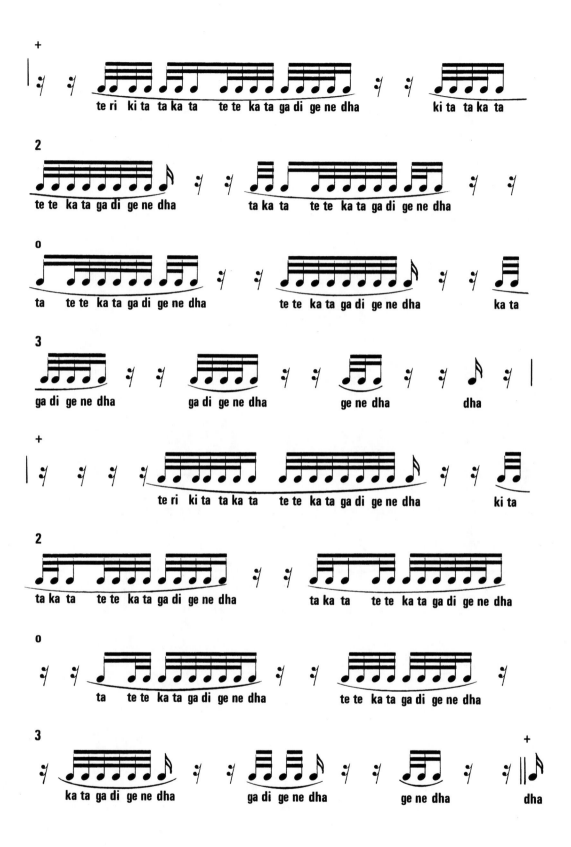

de re ki ta dha   ki ta   ta ka te ri   ki ta   ta ka de re de re

ki ta dha   ki ta   ta ka te ri   ki ta   ta ka de re de re ki ta dha

5.   MEDIUM EKTAL

te te   ka ta   ga di   ge ne   dha   te te   ka ta

ga di   ge ne   dha   te te   ka ta   ga di   ge ne   dha

B.   UNIVERSAL TIHAI FORMULA

All of the *tihais* that have been presented thus far as well as innumerable new ones may be derived from the following formula, of which there are two forms: one for *tihais* starting on *sam* and one for *tihais* starting elsewhere. The formula for *tihais* that start on *sam* is as follows:

$$G = \frac{(CTL + 1) - 3P}{2}$$, where G = the number of counts in the gap or rest between the *palas*, C = the

number of full cycles the *tihai* takes to return to the *sam*, T = the number of beats in one *tala* cycle, L = the number of subdivisions per beat (*laya*) and P = the number of counts in one *pala* of the *tihai*.

Both G and P must be expressed in terms of the *laya* used. For example, if the *tihai* is in *tigun laya* (three counts per beat), then the gap and *pala* must be counted using triplets. If the *tihai* is in *barabar laya* (one count per beat), then the gap and *pala* must be counted using the same units used to count the number of beats in the *tala*.

The formula works as follows:

To find the number of counts occupied by the gap, first find the number of counts that the *tihai* will last by multiplying the number of beats in one cycle of *tala* (T) by the number of cycles the *tihai* takes to return to *sam* (C) by the number of divisions or counts per beat (L) and adding one to the product to bring it to *sam*. Then subtract the total length of the *palas* (3P), and as there are two gaps divide the remainder by two to arrive at the number of counts in each gap.

Whew! So, if while performing one wants to create a *tihai*, one may take out a calculator and hope that the audience is still there and listening by the time the calculations are finished. But one shouldn't give up all hope, for the more *tihais* one learns, the more intuitive the process of spontaneous *tihai* creation becomes.

The formula can be used as follows:

If the *tala* is *rupak* (seven beats) and the *laya* is *tigun* (three counts per beat), then $G = \dfrac{(C \cdot 7 \cdot 3 + 1) - 3P}{2}$, insert-

ing 7 for T and 3 for L. Choosing a *pala* of 11 counts of three-per-beat *laya* divisions, $G = \dfrac{(C \cdot 7 \cdot 3 + 1) - 3 \cdot 11}{2}$.

As $7 \times 3 = 21$ and $3 \times 11 = 33$, it follows that $G = \dfrac{(C \cdot 21 + 1) - 33}{2}$. From this equation, it is obvious that C

(the number of cycles of *tala* the *tihai* takes to return to *sam*) cannot be one, as this would make G a negative num-

ber. Trying the next integer, one can see that if C $= 2$, then $G = \dfrac{(2 \cdot 21 + 1) - 33}{2}$. As this is equal to 10/2, G $= 5$.

Then one must assemble these mathematical facts into a *tihai*. The *tihai* starts on *sam*, is in *rupak tal* and is in a *laya* of three. The *pala* is eleven of these *laya* divisions in duration, with two gaps of five *laya* divisions each between the *palas*. Using syllables to represent the 11-count *palas*, the *tihai* can be written as follows:

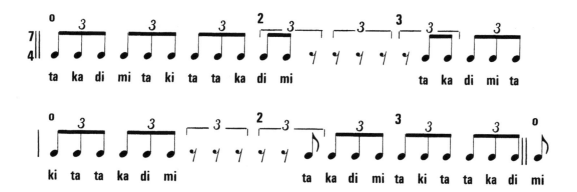

The formula can be modified slightly to create *tihais* that do not start on the *sam*. By adding L[(T + 1) - S], where S $=$ the number of the beat the *tihai* starts on (counting from the *sam* as the first beat), the additional fraction of a cycle caused by not starting on *sam* is added to the equation. Therefore, for *tihais* that do not start on *sam*, $G = \dfrac{[L(T + 1 - S) + (CTL + 1)] - 3P}{2}$. If the *tihai* is less than one cycle long, then C $= 0$, and if the *tihai* is X and a fraction cycles long, then the fraction is dropped and C $=$ X where X is an integer.

For example, one may use this formula to find the gap present for a *tihai* in *rupak tal* (seven beats) with a *laya* of three and a *pala* of 11 *laya* divisions, starting the *tihai* on the third beat of the *tala*. In this example, T $= 7$, L $= 3$, P $= 11$ and S $= 3$. Therefore, $G = \dfrac{[3(7 + 1 - 3) + C \cdot 7 \cdot 3 + 1] - 3 \cdot 11}{2}$ which can be further reduced to $G = \dfrac{(15 + C \cdot 21 + 1) - 33}{2}$. If C $= 1$, then $G = \dfrac{15 + 22 - 33}{2}$. Therefore, G $= 2$.

The resulting *tihai* starts on the third beat of *rupak tal*, is in *tigun laya*, and has a *pala* of 11 *laya* divisions and a gap of two *laya* divisions.

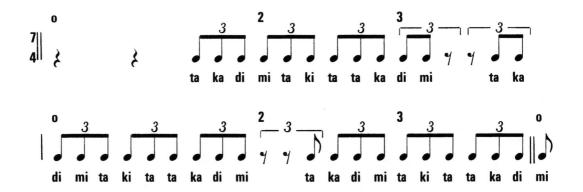

After going through a number of these calculations, one will find that the gap will sometimes be expressed as a fraction. If this is the case, the gap will be X + ½ *laya* divisions long (where X is an integer), which can make for some interesting, although tricky, *tihais*.

These formulas allow one to turn any phrase one likes into a *tihai* starting at any point in any *tala* by determining the proper gap length to make the *tihai* end on *sam*. Although the formulas require a number of intricate calculations, they are a versatile and useful tool for the construction of *tihais*.

C.   GREAT TIHAI FORMULA

For an instant *tihai* in any *tala*, this formula is offered: P = T - 1, where G = 2. If the *tala* is *jhaptal* (ten beats), then the *pala* length is nine beats. With a two-beat gap between *palas*, starting the *tihai* on *sam*, the resulting *tihai* returns to *sam* after three cycles of *jhaptal*.

D.   BHEDAM TIHAIS

A *tihai* is said to be *bhedam* (literally, "no breath") if there is no gap or breath between the *palas*. One must keep in mind, however, that *bhedam* is a relative term, as there is always an increment of time between any two consecutive notes. Generally speaking, a *tihai* may be considered *bhedam* if the distance between the beginning of the last note of the first *pala* and the first note of the second *pala* is equal to one increment of the prevailing *laya*, usually *chaugun*, or in faster speeds, *dugun*.

114

1.

"MAGIC NUMBER" TIHAI FORMULAS

A "magic number" is a numeral that when multiplied by three will equal a number of the *tala* cycles plus one count to return to *sam*. For example, the magic number for *tintal* is eleven, as $3 \times 11 = 33$, which is equal to two cycles of *tintal* plus one count. Magic numbers can be used to construct *tihais* with no gaps that start on *sam*. Not every *tala* has a corresponding magic number, for if the number of beats in a *tala* is equal to a multiple of three, no magic number exists and *sam-to-sam tihais* with no gaps are not possible.

The following formulas hold true:

$$P = \frac{\text{magic number}}{L} \text{ and } P = \frac{\text{magic number} + XTL}{L},$$ where P = the number of beats in the *pala*, X is an

integer greater than or equal to one, T = the number of beats in one cycle of *tala* (where T is not divisible by three), L = the number of subdivisions per beat (where L is not divisible by three), and the magic number is derived from TL (the number of *laya* divisions in one cycle of *tala*) using the accompanying table of magic numbers.

T × L	MAGIC NUMBER	T × L	MAGIC NUMBER	T × L	MAGIC NUMBER
4	3	43	29	80	27
5	2	44	15	82	55
7	5	46	31	83	28
8	3	47	16	85	57
10	7	49	33	86	29
11	4	50	17	88	59
13	9	52	35	89	30
14	5	53	18	91	61
16	11	55	37	92	31
17	6	56	19	94	63
19	13	58	39	95	32
20	7	59	20	97	65
22	15	61	41	98	33
23	8	62	21	100	67
25	17	64	43	101	34
26	9	65	22	103	69
28	19	67	45	104	35
29	10	68	23	106	71
31	21	70	47	107	36
32	11	71	24	109	73
34	23	73	49	110	37
35	12	74	25	112	75
37	25	76	51	113	38
38	13	77	26	115	77
40	27	79	53	116	39
41	14				

Tihais without gaps that do not start on *sam* can be created in any *tala* by utilizing the formula $S = CT + 2 - 3P$, where S = the number of the beat the *tihai* starts on counting from *sam* as the first beat, C = the number of cycles occupied by the *tihai* rounded up to the nearest integer (2½ cycles would be counted as three), T = the number of beats in the *tala*, and P = the number of beats in the *pala*.

Utilize these formulas to create original *tihais*.

F.   CHAKKRADARS

Generally speaking, a *chakkradar* is a style of *tabla* composition played three times and timed to end on *sam*. Often the *tabla* composition itself ends in a *tihai*, in which case the whole composition including the *tihai* is played three times.

1.   BHEDAM CHAKKRADAR IN MEDIUM SLOW TINTAL

This composition was written by the renowned *tabla* master, Alla Rakha.

117

G.   FORMAISHI TIHAIS

A *formaishi tihai* is a *tabla* composition ending with a *tihai*. The entire composition is played three times. The first time through the composition the first *pala* of the *tihai* ends on *sam*; the second time through, the second *pala* of the *tihai* ends on *sam*; and the last time through, the third *pala* of the *tihai* ends on *sam*.

1.

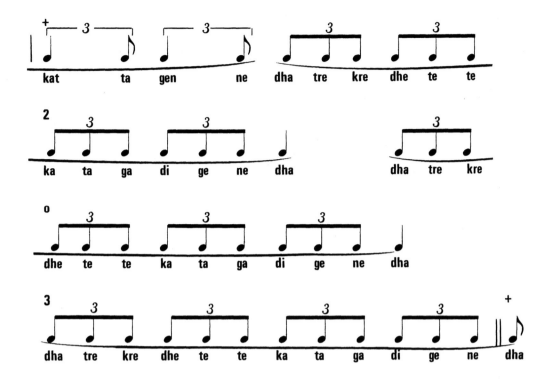

2.   FORMAISHI TIHAI FORMULA

This formula will produce *formaishi tihais* in any *tala* in which the number of beats in one cycle of the *tala* minus one is divisable by three producing an integer, such as *rupak* (seven beats), *jhaptal* (ten beats) and *tintal* (16 beats). It assumes a *laya* of one. The number of beats occupied by the part of the *formaishi tihai* composition before the internal *tihai* is equal to the magic number for the *tala* plus one (magic number + 1). One *pala* of the internal *tihai* is equal to one-third of the difference between the number of beats in the *tala* and one, or $\frac{T-1}{3}$. The length of the entire internal *tihai* is equal to three times this, the result of which is equal to the number of beats in the *tala* minus one (T - 1). The length of one repetition of the entire *formaishi tihai* composition is equal to the magic number plus one plus the number of beats in the *tala* minus one.

The following formula is therefore used:

$$F = \underbrace{\text{first part of composition}}_{\text{magic number} + 1} + \underbrace{\text{internal } \textit{tihai}}_{3 \cdot \frac{(T-1)}{3}}$$

where f = the number of beats in one repetition of the *formaishi tihai* composition, *laya* = 1, and $\frac{T-1}{3}$ is an integer.

ārdhā lāya: one half speed.

ārdhā jaitāl: 6½-beat *tala*.

ārhai lāya: 2½ speed.

ārī: one-half.

ātgun lāya: octuple speed.

barābar: equal.

barābar lāya: normal speed.

bhēdam tihai: *tihai* without rests between the repetitions.

bōls: syllables of the *tabla* drum language. Each syllable represents a sound on the drums.

chāchar tāl: 14-beat *tala*.

chakkradār: composition generally ending with a *tihai*, repeated three times and timed to end on the *sam*.

chand: phrasing of counts into groups.

chārtāl kī sawārī tāl: 11-beat *tala*.

chaugun lāya: quadruple speed.

chēgun lāya: sextuple speed.

chōwtāl: 12-beat *tala*.

dādra tāl: six-beat *tala*.

deri lāya: 1½ speed.

dhammār tāl: 14-beat *tala*.

drut: fast speed.

dūgun: double speed.

ēktāl: 12-beat *tala*.

fōrmaishī tihai: thrice-repeated *tabla* composition ending with a *tihai*. The first time through, the first *pala* of the *tihai* ends on *sam*; the second time, the second *pala* of the *tihai* ends on *sam*; the third time, the third *pala* ends on *sam*.

Hindūstānī music: form of music prevailing in North India.

jaitāl: 13-beat *tala*.

jhāptāl: ten-beat *tala*.

kehārwa tāl: eight-beat *tala*.

khālī: literally, the "empty" beat, it is an unaccented beat of the *tala*, secondary in importance only to the *sam*, and is marked by a wave of the hands.

kwārī: three-quarter after.

lāya: speed; either the tempo of the *tala* or the speed relative to the *tala*; in the later form it can refer to the divisions of the beat.

madhya: medium speed.

mātra: unit of measurement of musical time, equivalent to a beat.

nōgun lāya: ninefold speed.

pala: one "leg" or part of a *tihai*, the *pala* is played three times.

pānchgun lāya: quintuple speed.

pāō lāya: one-quarter speed.

paunē dō lāya: 1¾ speed.

paunē chār lāya: 3¾ speed.

paunē tin lāya: 2¾ speed.

paun lāya: three-quarter speed.

rūpak tāl: seven-beat *tala*.

sam: the first beat of the *tala*, marked by a clap of the hands, it is the most heavily accented beat of the *tala*.

sārhē tin lāya: 3½ speed.

sātgun lāya: septuple speed.

sawai: one-quarter after.

sawai dō lāya: 2¼ speed.

sawai lāya: 1¼ speed.

sawai tin lāya: 3¼ speed.

sawārī tāla: a type of *tala* containing two or more groupings of 1½ beats, causing an irregular rhythm pattern.

sitārkhānī tāl: 16-beat *tala*.

tabla: a pair of drums with goat-skin heads, the primary percussion instrument of North India.

tāl: a rhythmic cycle.

tāla: same as *tal*, this sanskrit pronunciation is often shortened to *tal* in North India.

tālī: a marker of *tala* rendered by a hand clap.

thēka: a standard set of *bols* that identifies a particular *tala*.

tigun lāya: triple speed.

tihai: a rhythmic phrase repeated three times, usually timed to end on *sam*.

tintāl: 16-beat *tala*, the most common of all the *talas*.

upa dāsī tāl: 10½-beat *tala*.

vilambit: slow speed.

PRONUNCIATION GUIDE TO TRANSLITERATION

SYMBOL	PRONUNCIATION
ā	as in *saw, star*
a	as in *up, tub*
ī	as in *key, feet*
i	as in *pin, him*
ū	as in *room, food*
u	as in *put, pull*
ē	as in *egg, day*
e	as in *test*
ō	as in *so, foe*
ai	as in *eye, Thailand*
au	as in *crow*
ch	as in *chase*, avoid aspiration
dh	aspirated *d*
jh	aspirated *j*
jn	*gy* pronounced simultaneously
mr	*mr* pronounced simultaneously
śr	as in *shrine*
th	aspirated *t*
ty	*ty* pronounced simultaneously
dhy	aspirated *d* and *y* pronounced simultaneously
r	in between the English *r* and *d*

SECTION II

FUTURE POSSIBILITIES

CHAPTER 4

FUTURE POSSIBILITIES

The possibilities for creative development through the application of the knowledge presented in this work are vast. Through studying the rhythms of the worlds great traditions, one gains an improved sense of the basic elements of rhythm that will help one to play any form of music. Imagine the freshness of approach knowledge of these world rhythms could bring to the improvisations of a jazz musician, the added confidence and scope this knowledge could give to a rock musician, and the accuracy of rhythmic delivery a symphonic player could achieve. The knowledge of the world's traditions points to exciting possibilities for the composer and improvising musician to create new forms of music.

Think of the range of musical possibilities created by combining ideas from different traditions. The mind travels to concepts such as *tihai kotèkans* (gained through combining rhythmic elements of North India and Bali), multiple layers of rhythm in odd metric cycles (African rhythm combined with Indian *tala*), multiple layers of *kotèkans* (African rhythm combined with Balinese interlocking parts), and multiple layers of *kotèkans* in odd metric cycles (African rhythm combined with Balinese interlocking parts and Indian *tala*). One can compose melodies and harmonies to these rhythms, using them as spark for the creative fire.

The exercises presented here are intended as examples of some of the new and exciting possibilities that are available for exploration. It is hoped that they will inspire ideas for original exercises to enhance one's own form of musical expression.

EXERCISE I

This exercise was developed by utilizing *kotèkan* cards, *tabla bols*, and the Universal *Tihai* Formula. It is in a 15-beat rhythmic cycle. Recite the *tabla bols* while keeping *tal*, starting first with the *polos* part (the bottom part) and then proceeding to the *nyangsih* part (the top and more offbeat part). Once these are mastered, perform them as a *kotèkan* with a partner.

After studying this example, create *tihai kotèkans* in various different *talas* utilizing the *kotèkan* cards and the Universal *Tihai* Formula. Compose melodies for the *kotèkans*, or fill in the rhythms with *tabla bols, solkattu* or *Eve* drum syllables.

TIHAI/KOTEKAN

128

EXERCISE II

This exercise utilizes African rhythms in conjunction with South Indian *solkattu*. The *solkattu* syllables were taken directly from Exercise IV of the South Indian section of this work. In fact, the entire *tisra gati* section of that exercise can be played against the African bell pattern. This exercise requires at least three participants.

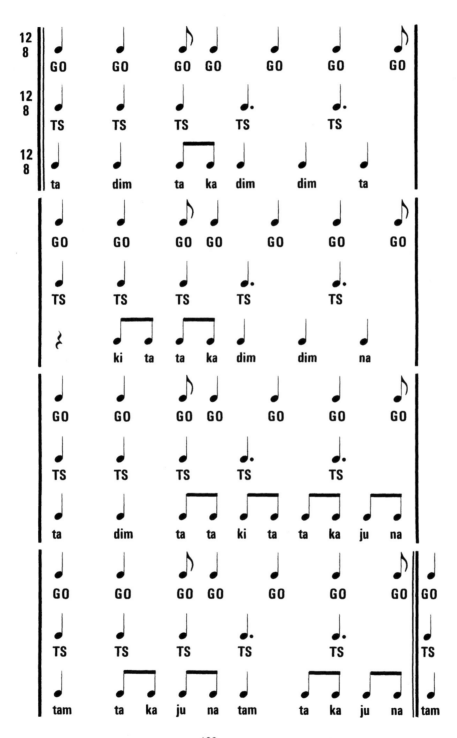

EXERCISE III

This exercise utilizes African bell and rattle patterns in conjunction with a *kotèkan*. Melodic figures were composed for the rhythms, and where the parts meet care was taken to make sure a suitable harmony occurred. This exercise requires four melodic instruments or voices.

Try creating original exercises using African rhythms in conjunction with *kotèkans*.

CONCLUSION

Create original fusion exercises by combining the rhythmic concepts of Africa, Bali, India and any other tradition previously studied. This process can be quite interesting and fun, and can teach one something about composition. Keep in mind, though, that the result of such experiments can often sound forced. To create music which truly expresses one's unique personality, one may guide the composition from one's deepest and most sincere feelings, and let the synthesis of musical knowledge happen in the subconscious mind. This is not to downplay the importance of these exercises, for not only do they help one to see and experience new possibilities, they may even provide the spark for a sudden moment of inspiration. In the initial euphoria inspired by these creations, be careful to steer clear of the temptation to show only the most basic common ground between traditions, for this is a road to stagnation through loss of diversity. The idea of world fusion music is to create new art forms to exist alongside the old, and in so doing bring more diversity to music.

Be creative, improvise and compose! New ground may be broken in world fusion music, inspiring others to take a look at the unique wisdom and knowledge each culture on earth possesses. Perhaps by showing that ideas from separate cultures can work together in harmony, musicians can point a way towards the fulfillment of mankind's dream of global understanding.

BIBLIOGRAPHY

Chernoff, John Miller. *African Rhythm and African Sensibility*. Chicago: University of Chicago Press, 1979.

Ekweme, L. *Ibo Choral Music—Its Theory and Practice*. Yale University Ph.D., 1972.

Hamel, Peter Michael. *Through Music to the Self*. London: Compton Press, 1978.

Holyroyde, Peggy. *The Music of India*. New York: Praeger Publishers, 1972.

Issac, L. Theory of Indian Music. Madras: Shyam Printers, 1967.

Jones, A.M. *Studies in African Music*, vols. 1-2. London: Oxford University Press, 1957.

Khan, Sufi Inayat. *Music*. New Delhi: The Sufi Publishing Company, 1962.

Ladzekpo, S. Kobla and Pantaleoni, Hewitt. "*Takada* Drumming," *African Music, Journal of the African Music Society*, vol. 4, no. 4, 6-31.

McPhee, Colin, *Music in Bali*. New Haven and London: Yale University Press, 1966.

Nketia, J.H. Kwabena. *The Music of Africa*. New York: W.W. Norton and Company, 1974.

Popley, Herbert A. *The Music of India*. New Delhi: Y.M.C.A. Publishing House, 1966.

Reck, David. *Music of the Whole Earth*. New York: Charles Scribner's Sons, 1977.

Sambamoorthy, P. *South Indian Music*, vols. 1-7. Madras: The Indian Music Publishing House, n.d.

Shankar, Ravi. *My Music, My Life*. New York: Simon and Schuster, 1968.

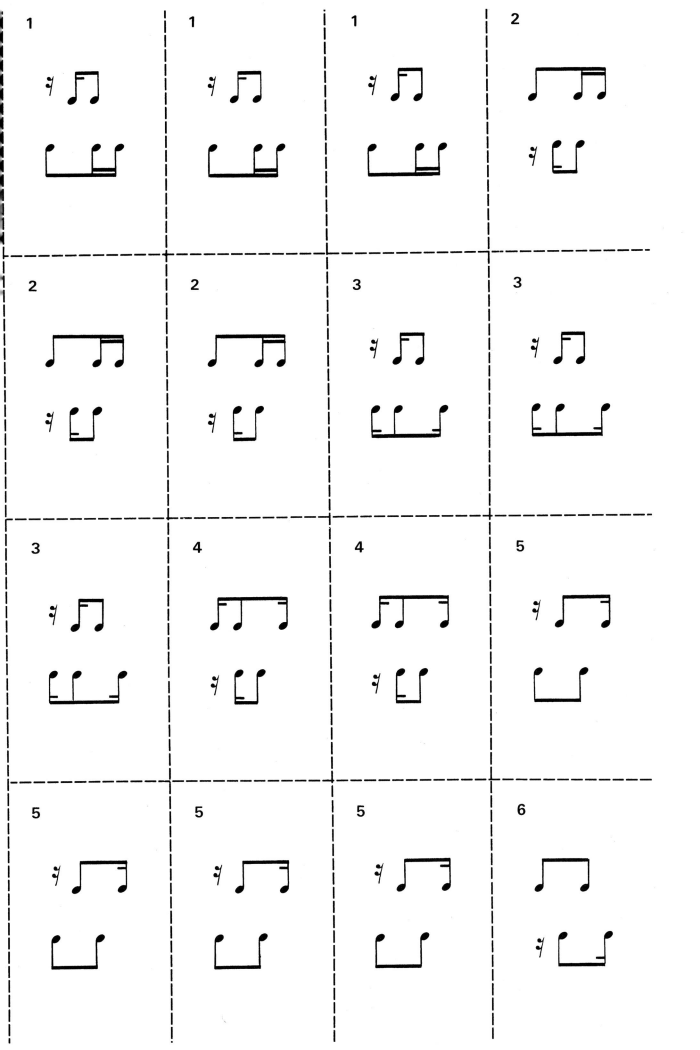

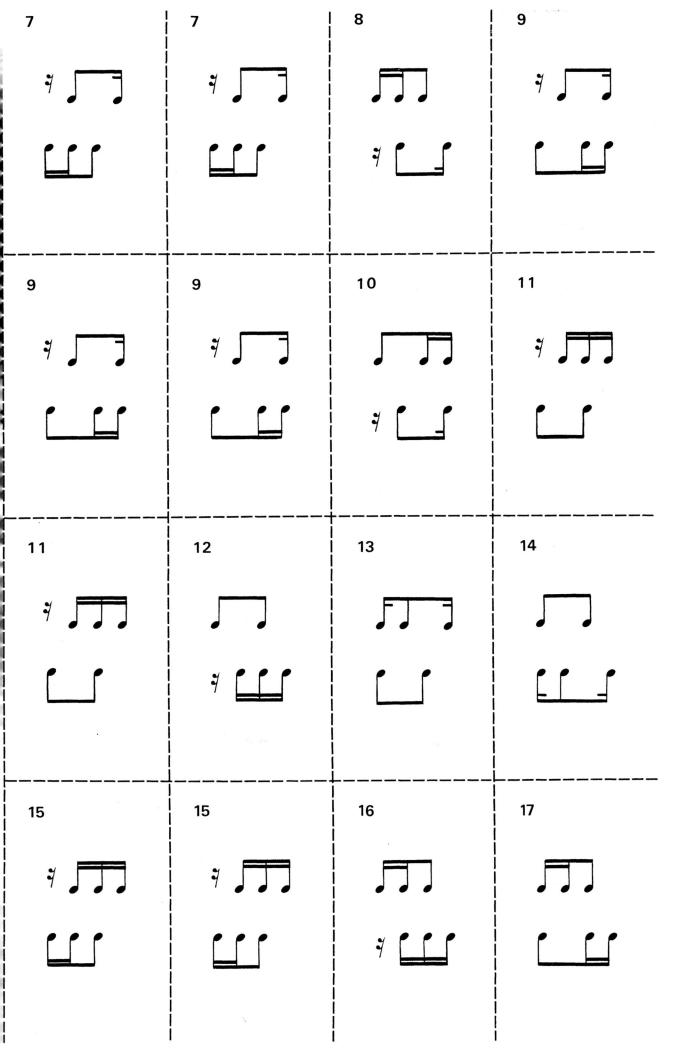

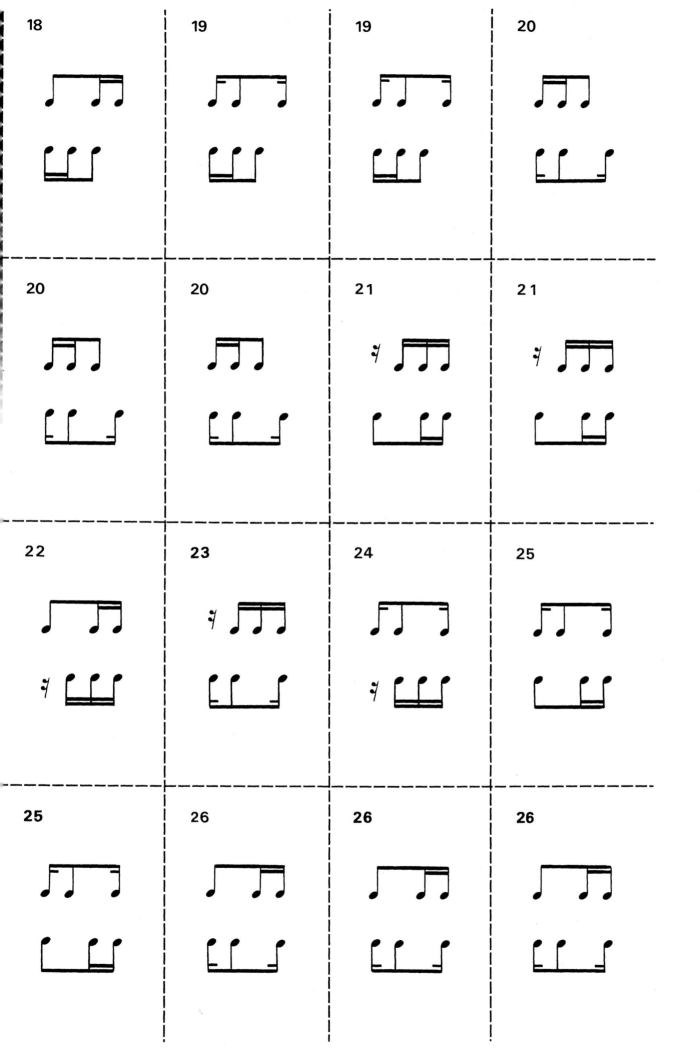